DEVIL'S ERUDITION

DARIN GRAVES

Devil's Erudition
Copyright © 2021 by Darin Graves

All rights reserved. No part of this publication may be reproduced, distributed, or transmitted in any form or by any means, including photocopying, recording, or other electronic or mechanical methods, without the prior written permission of the author, except in the case of brief quotations embodied in critical reviews and certain other non-commercial uses permitted by copyright law.

ISBN
978-1-956161-35-9 (Hardcover)
978-1-956161-34-2 (Paperback)
978-1-956161-33-5 (eBook)

TABLE OF CONTENTS

Devil's Erudition 1
Mick 13
Kill Shot 27
The Prosecutor 37
Zoonosis 47
The Majestic Lyricist 51
Castle Bravo 55
Trapper's Purgatory 65
The Choice 73
Ethics? 79
Primordial Instincts 91
Presence 95
Counterpart 105
They Call Him "Leather Apron" 109
Devil And Father 121
Confliction 127

DEVIL'S ERUDITION

Darin Graves

DEEP, DEEP SPACE. IT IS SOMETIMES thought that the big bang brought forward the beginning of life, the beginning of matter within space. All matter burst violently as a result of rapid combustion, typically scattering fragments wildly across the void. As matter spread, chunks of elements, small as a grain of sand, big as a small moon, violently crashed and collided into each other, mixing their magnetic resonance into different chains. Before that bang, the matter was condensed into a small, by comparison, sphere called a black hole. As the internal parts of elements expanded, a thing we call gravitation expanded.

The amount of elements is massive, to say the least; as time went by, a million galaxies were created. The violent and destructive shattering of the bang plus the immense pull and push of gravity in effect showered materials to form galaxies in a spiral array. A gravitational wave is made when massive amounts of matter, traveling three-quarters the speed of light, feel gravity from nearby materials, changing their pathway into circular strides. Before the black hole fulminates debris, when it is small to the point moving matter can still escape its grasp, it needs an event horizon to take place. It grows to the point that its gravitation will not allow matter, light, and gamma radiation to flee. At the event horizon is finally maintained, the hole still gains gravitational pull, although it no longer needs it.

Gravitation is the key to this entire spectrum. Thick areas of space are filled with globular clusters. There are five hundred million galaxies, each made from their own black hole that grows over millions of years in the galaxy's center. Each, not all, of the galaxies, take on a flat two-dimensional disk. Angular momentum, by gravitational pull, spirals constitutions in a circular momentum making the galaxy flat. The same thing happens with the million universes within the galaxy. Star in the middle with planets in a circular position; they all go in the same orbit around the sun, all making a frisbee rotation. Each galaxy has its own black hole, taking billions of years to collide materials until the big bang happens again.

Time itself exists only with matter; space has nothing to do with time. There would be no tomorrow without a planet circling a sun. Yet space, time, and matter are evolved in making things as they are. Space is in a world all its own; it is not a predictable plot, the human mind cannot come up with a fathomable proposal or intention for the simple fact that it never ends. All these scientific truths are natural, quite established by our father. All galaxies in the seeable void contain stars, asteroids, planets, and galactic clouds, their biggest difference is that most are elliptical, but some are irregular in their spirals.

Again, our solar system is a gravitationally bound system; gravity controls any mystery, controls the entire shape and consistency of matter in all galaxies. Our galaxy is 100,000 light-years across and contains 100 billion stars. The location of humans on earth goes to the solar system, milky way galaxy, local galactic group, Virgo supercluster, local superclusters, and finally, the observable universe, beyond which we have never seen. It can only be said once space goes on forever, there is no end.

Back to our solar system, we have eight planets and a dwarf or two, Pluto and Charon. Our system is located in the Orion arm of the milky way; our orbits are nearly circular and have an orbital eccentricity. The theory core accretion has smaller planets have the heat of the sun drive off-gases and vapors where outer planets contain gas vapors, more towards its core do you find solid matter. Our solar system is the gravitationally bound system that has its sun and objects that orbit it, and it is 4.6 billion years old. The four smaller inner planets, called "terrestrial planets," are primarily composed of rock and metal. The four outer planets, known as "gas giants," are substantially larger and more massive than the inner ones. Most contain a moon or many moons. The planet called Earth was formed by space gas, dust, chunks of matter, and other galactic materials. In the beginning, 4.5 billion years ago, the rotation around the sun began to collect water from comets and asteroids; the rocky nucleus accreted dust and debris leftover from the formation of the sun. Father could quite easily see this was the planet he had been looking for. Water was pure, not icy glaciers or gas, perfect rotation around the sun; this planet was perfect for life through clear, pure water. Father thought of several different creation myths. A symbolic narrative of the beginning of the world as understood in a particular tradition of science knowledge. Evolution is the change of heritable characteristics of biological populations over successive generations and genes passed from parent to offspring. Evolution occurs when evolutionary processes such as natural selection and genetic drift act on this variation, resulting in certain characteristics becoming more dominant and naturally more common within the population. Bacteria were starting to show in a violent storm, where survival was against you. Through evolution, as millions of years went by, cells began combining into more significant life forms, fossils started leaving their mark 3 billion years ago. Homo Erectus, through different timescales, used evolution to advance; survival was difficult and hard to exist. But evolution is there to advance your percentage to survive. As millions of years went by, the meek were left to perish as only the advanced animals would survive. It has nothing to do with the creation of life. Evolution is nature's way to advance newborns from their parents, surviving at a high cost, but the actual immediate creation of life itself was given from the father. Evolution deals with a living structure, but that living structure exists through a more heavenly body, the father. The father does have no idea of time; everything simply exists. The Orion arm of the milky way, the father, found a planet that could contain biotic components with water as its prime. This solar system had a planet perfectly fit within the spectrum for liquid water, so the father created life! Life is a circle of momentum; it exists on the edge, any faltering changes could lead it to demise, its destruction. Each circle is a year-long, as evolution controls who carries the genes fit for survival. Small organisms, as millions of years, go by, develop into larger bodies. It was a very small start which leads to an entire planet full of life! Life went across entire continents, evolution past the years, in balance with nature, made different creatures small and large, solidifying their future as their young were fitter than their parents through the survival process. The father watched and watched as various organisms took the lead. The father knew his evolution was coming along perfectly; through Homo Erectus, human taxonomy is designed to include both anatomically modern humans and extinct varieties as man evolved from archaic humans. Homo Erectus to Homo Sapiens Idaltu! The father was fascinated to watch them grow; their central nervous systems, the cerebral cortex through time and evolution, increased in mass and included 15 billion neurons! As time went by, all human beings started experiencing anger, jealousy, sadness, frustration, and irritation. Watching them grow was astonishing; evolution was taking them closer to the father himself, much more like him, but they were not puppets more so than not. He could often only witness and change things if he felt so, but their future was sometimes their own. Their emotions ruled at times rather than common sense, like a puppet flung by the swing of a pendulum. Father watched as time went by. The size of the planet took different populations, their DNA, to different areas of the planet. Continents had different people. Father was happy to analyze and study Homo Erectus. The one creature in this sphere of clay and silt who advanced among all brutal beasts. Father gave them a look like his own, human. This planet will be a circular display of life, perfect distance from its sun, water will be clear, plants will grow at first, then the animals will take shape, using evolution within its DNA to advance towards mental sublimity! But flawlessness will take time! Toward the beginning of Earth, the heat will be immense, and volcanic eruptions will take place, distancing the continents and placing beds of smooth granite to fill oceans. Rives will be the bloodline, the veins, to bring water to the flora and all vegetation. Father liked what he saw, but will the saints? Father knew that conditions necessary for life to begin were breathable air, moderate temperature and climate, water, and available food. Flora and vegetation would have to be done first before any living entity. It took Father less than a second to create Heterotrophs, the first beginners of life on earth, inhabiting the sea and absorbing the organic material that was being created by the reactions of the earth, amino acids. They are the building blocks of the radical headstones of life. Father knew that evolution would follow as first life took hold, from atom to cells, cells to organs, organs to animals. Again, a circular display of life moving forward. It would take billions of years to conclude, but Father did not care of time; he always has been and always will be. Father always thought, concluded, that the Saints will accept this form of life. All existing creatures will enjoy this outcome, this sequel of life, and this incredible effect of creation. As time went by, the Saints will know of this creation, this formation designed by Father they will accept. Will any of them defy my grace? The humans will expand and spread their own entity and will develop souls. They will go beyond animals, mere beasts, modeling, fashioning, epitomizing their flesh into souls!

The Fathers' thought of awareness, through experience, told him he would be denied his grace, his love for man. One of the Angels, the Saints, will not accept his love and grace for humans, is man as good as the Saints? Father thought, yes, my love will never end. Father knew there was resistance in accepting these people, and he could sense a presence coming this way. Father was now looking over the earth; he loved the beauty and charm earth had in its orbit; he very rapidly went to another space of alluring and angelic sites in our solar system, Saturn; he loved looking at its rings. Father loved the sheer aspiration of the gape of Saturn; the demeanor gave him peace and wisdom. Father billowed in the beauty and saw a small curly pink sphere right outside the rings.

"Hello Father,...I knew you would be here. You adore these little planets look," said Lucifer. Father never replied; he usually kept silent unless there was something to say.

"You, of course, we're looking over those tiny snobs on earth." Lucifer had told Father many times how he felt betrayed. He had for so many years tried to let other Saints join him on this charade, this revolt against what Father has done, but he was always by himself.

"Do you love me, father?"

"Of course I do, more than you shall ever know."

"Then why do you do this?" Lucifer almost screamed. "Oh, that's right, you love them too."

Father never needed to answer that question.

"I witnessed how you created this planet," Lucifer stated, "I knew of your creation longer than you think, evolutionary strain and all of that, these creatures, these piglets, could gain tenfold as time goes by a question for you Father, evolution is not creation, these piglets, are creating scientists whose plan to know the universe, yet all they have to do is look at their own solar system. How could they look at their own earth and compare it to other planets? This Saturn, Venus, Mercury, all of them do not have anything close to hold life; water would be chunks or vapor, mixed with other elements." Lucifer, as he said this, was almost screaming. "These piglets mock you, Father, you created their existence, give them tools, watch them grow, elite intelligent presence yet they mock you, become atheists. They go to their moon, dream of going to other planets, yet those planets would kill them in a heartbeat. Their solar system, the only one planet of life that they are on, is like no other. Their imagination, their dream of living on other planets is just that, a dream." Lucifer screamed, "Evolution is not creation; those atheists ignore you and do not realize you created them at the beginning."

Lucifer had told this many times to father before; he thought it was a waste of time. He changed his attitude, became calm. "Father," he said calmly, "I saw how you took water from Mars; there used to be an ocean on it, oh but Earth needed it, right Father. There were other elements you took from planets and put on Earth," Lucifer giggled.

Father came out of his silence, "Speaking of elements, there is a portion on Earth which I did not want there, on their table of elements, Uranium. Lucifer, you put it there, didn't you."

"Uranium……..oh no, not me," Lucifer giggled. "Why would I do that?"

There was silence for several seconds, "OK, just a bit."

"A bit, 10 million tons," Father said.

"How else would they build nuclear plants? I have given them the ability for good clean power," he replied.

"Also the ability to kill themselves," replied Father.

"Father, through evolution, they have become predators, and you blame me?. A hand becomes a fist, and rock becomes a hammer, a stick becomes an arrow, a branch becomes a spear,...the creation of gunpowder.... it goes on and on. Their wars are inevitable."

Father kept quiet because he knew Lucifer was right.

"That brings me to another question, the demeanor of these humans is questionable.

I have seen, and you have seen, their greed, more often than not, goes beyond helping one another. Each man wants, desires, and craves economic favors before he would worry about another human being. You can't go to the hospital unless,..unless you have insurance. Vanity is my favorite sin. You know Father, I believe I know them more than you. They see themselves as faithful, caring people; they go to church, love holidays, give to charities, help other people at times, but that's a charade! They would give up their divine faith in you, Father, if they lost their massive income. They would like their green bills before you, Father; why don't you just admit it!"

There was a moment of silence, a few seconds later, Lucifer continued, raising his voice, "I have been with these piglets longer than you, I have been here when the whole thing started, I became one of them, remember Father, when you sliced off my wings and threw me into the dismal void, I ended up on earth as you thought I betrayed you, NO, you betrayed me," he was screaming, "I cannot Father, cannot see how you put these piglets can be looked at with the Saints, just as good as us really?"

There was another moment of silence. "Shall we talk about these creatures from a psychological point of view? Why don't we stay with his sins, this evolutionary fold you have made for him, the instincts, give him every chance to sin and betray you continually. The Saints gave up on this a thousand years ago, but these humans are right in the middle of it. Greed, sloth, gluttony, lust, wrath, envy, and pride, a million fold of humans reaching for the same thing and destroying each other getting it, sin after sin after sin, trying to make themselves better! I cannot see how you are not sickened by it, Father."

The sun was giving Saturn a golden glow. The space around them went forever, never stopping. Many of its moons gave off a radiance, a luminosity of white and red lights.

Lucifer knew his thoughts, how he felt about humans, and telling Father of misconceptions was not waste; Father must be reminded.

"When I first was thrown into the chasm, after I let you know the dark series of the piglet's sins, I still had power but was inserted into their situation, their way of living. The same thing happened to Jesus, your son. Behold and remember, Father." Lucifer felt this was necessary. "Then Jesus, being filled with the Holy Spirit, returned from Jordan and was led by the Spirit into the wilderness, being tempted 40 days and 40 nights by the devil. And in those days, he ate nothing, and afterward, when they had ended, he was hungry."

"I thought that threw his starvation, he would fall, but no, he circled himself in the clay, into the soil and reasoned. I would really know what he thought, but I could not sense him. The desert, sand, water is scarce, a few plants and wind. The day I saw Jesus enter the barren estate, this province trial of survival, I could not help but smile. I would have to give him a visit,....yes I did, Father,...yes I did."

Father had a beam in his look, a smirk, his own son being tested when through his faith should not be tested at all.

"But how should I test this man?" Lucifer cried out loud. "He was a man or something more?" Several seconds went by. "When my wings were sliced, Father, I almost felt like one of these pigs, walking, talking, breathing...everything. Was Jesus the same? No,..his faith was....clear..... ratified completely pure! I am a humanist; in a way, what could I offer to him to take his unadulterated, authentic and perfect faith from you Father, what?"

There was silence for a moment. As they looked around, a million stars could be seen. Space did not seem like a void; there was something there; they could feel it.

"I slithered to him like a snake; the question in my mind was what would tempt him; he is a human, is he not? Bare women willing, terracotta jars full of wine, pillared house with servants to please you.....yes I know Father, I am just starting. As the days went by, I came to him as a lizard. I told him he could be the ruler of the land, all humankind, all ethnic groups, the entire nation will be at his feet. All you see could be at your waning all of it."

Lucifer told Father, "This was a time I had to take advantage of...... but what good would it do? His faith was pure.....Who was in authority in the presence of God, he said. Your faith will take you there, Lucifer the scriptures and prophets will know. His resistance to my embracing of faith was exhaustively complete. He stood unbreakable."

Father and Lucifer looked at each other, never blinking. "As the weeks went by, I crawled to him as a scorpion, challenged him, told him if he only knew what he would become if he switches his faith. I must help my brother, he said. Under the presence of God and the sanctuary of the land, Love the Lord your God with all your heart and with all your soul and with all your mind and with all your strength I was besieged."

The last days Jesus was in the desert, I told him, "Until an opportune time."

"He could almost feel his own fate......crucified, in retribution, I made sure Pontius Pilate was in a disagreeable mood. Do what you do best to this questionable beetle."

"If I cannot break your faith,...I will break your body," Lucifer cried, "Three days after his crucifixion, he flew to you, Father."

There was a long moment of silence; Father said, "You always remind me that I sliced your wings off, you should analyze yourself, Saint Lucifer..... you used to be one of the kindest Saints around....then you found the humans, the ethics, the people who must be able to find themselves half the time, yes, you are right....they sin they think of themselves before they think of others, bad decisions are made consistently. They must learn as they continue in time; they are not flawless. As time goes by, they will make up for their mistakes, I wish you could see that, but you don't." Father said this very calmly. Lucifer's reaction was not so even.

"I call them pigs because that is what they are," said Lucifer yelling. "Self inclined, greedy piglets who would not care for others just as long as they make their fortunes. I have demons who are very busy in taking care of Purgatory; you know me, Father, all of my demons are occupied in applying punishment for those who will be going to heaven. Not one demon I have can possess a human; they are too busy. I have been with these creatures from the very beginning. If you have seen what I have seen, you would not be so forgiving. Stealing, all the time, robbery, oh yes, I cannot believe you gave them souls for when their body dies.

This evolution you have created for them is an imitation, an almost forgery, to live their lives sinning....and still go to heaven. Have you ever wondered, Father, they could live their lives in sin, stabbing their brothers in the back, believe in the resurrection of Jesus Christ, and still get to heaven? My demons administer their damnation by making sure they understand the punishment Jesus went through in his life, not just crucifixion, his entire life!" screamed Lucifer.

Father was still calm; Lucifer still thinks his point would not come through, no matter how many facts he throws at Father. "You know as much as I do, Father, that these piglets... murder one another for pleasure. There is a point inside their minds which they cannot concede, of killing each other for sport," Lucifer giggled. "Not one of them will ever go to heaven. I will see to it. Their thoughts, their actions are carried on by themselves, the evolution they go through, the instincts, their predisposition they act on is done without my supervision. Father, I am not a puppeteer; I merely wallow their desires; I sometimes lead them in the opposite direction, although what they aspire to is the reason they are there in the first place. They have no one to blame but themselves."

They stared at each other, "Do you believe me, Father, they call me the devil...yet all of their sins, all their tricking traps, the times they would give so much but get back very little astonishes me, the average man is easily taken, easily tricked, and their soul is easily confiscated. It is not my fault, and their desires are unstoppable... I merely set the stage. The orchestra is playing. Can you dance?"

They stared at each other; the black darkness which laid in space was as cold as Lucifers' heart. "Jesus faith won't change Father...neither will mine." Father knew, still had optimism in this world he created. Father said, "They will learn from their past; I wish you could see the light."

"I have spent many years of my life observing, viewing them..... develop. Your optimism would be pessimism if you would see it through my eyes," Lucifer added, "think of it as my...Erudition...my own scholarship as they advance. Unlike you, I can give individuals a minute of my time, talk to them. There are many atheists....and many Devil worshippers among them. I learn more about them every day. Oh, so many stories."

MICK

Written by Darin Graves

SERIAL KILLER EXPLANATION

I kill her, and I will be fulfilled
But it never happens........
So, next woman, I will be fulfilled, But it never happens.......
So, kill again, I will be fulfilled...
But it never happens. Another girl.....
Another girl.....
Another girl.....
It will go on until I am stopped simply because.....
I will never be fulfilled!
Before the kill, I will be fulfilled, I think I will but by history, but I Won't.......

Ted Bundy

Florida State Penitentiary. A couple of weeks before execution.

    A serial killer is typically by law, a person who kills three or more people. Much of the psychological profile was made from conversations with Ted Bundy. Mental gratification is the usual motive for multiple killings. It really does not matter what the FBI's psychological motive is;

what does matter is it will never stop. The serial profile varies for different killers, but the real point is that, no matter what reason, the killings will never stop until he is arrested or killed.

Mick finally got a date with Melissa. He had been in contact with her for years; they knew each other for a long time through different friends, although they went to different high schools. It was the summer before they both went to college, they were going to a different association, but both academic societies were in the same city, so they were excited. Mick knew to keep the date hush-hush; fewer people knew of any relationship, the better. He told her he was going to make supper for her and they would watch some cd movies afterward, told her over the phone to tell her parents that she was going out with friends, be back whenever she did just that.

Mick looked out of the front window and saw Melissa's car pull up, he thought. "Her car.. have to take care of that later." He watched her walk up to the front door; he looked around as best he could to see if anyone was watching, he saw no one. His mom went to see her sister this weekend, so she would be gone the whole week. He quickly remembered when his mom and dad divorced when he was a kid, the loud arguments, and dad slapped mom several times. He felt useless for not helping mom, but at the time, he somehow felt it was not his problem. Mellisa looked very good as she walked up to the front door, with long blond hair, a white t-shirt, and blue jeans with legs torn off. Awesome.

"Hi Missy," he opened the door for her without knocking and quickly got her into the house.

"Hey Mick," she came in and put her purse on the coat hangers, and took her shoes off. "Oooh, smells good."

"I already cooked the chicken and potatoes, just waiting for the green beans to warm up," he responded.

"You said before your mom is out of town." "Yes, she went to see my aunt Charlene."

"Great," Melissa said.

Mark was happy with the way things were going. They walked back to the kitchen, and Mellisa sat at the kitchen table. "This smells good...I am starving."

Mark filled two plates with food and brought them over to the table. "I think you will love this chicken, extra mushroom sauce, special recipe. A quick question, what did you tell your parents what you are doing tonight?"

"I told them I was going out with Shawna and her friends," they gazed at each other and half-smiled. They were thinking of adult things. They both had supper and chatted about adolescent, youthful things, their future, and dreams of a world open and ready for their generation. What they wanted to be and how they saw the world. They spoke and contemplated their aspirations while in the back of their minds wondering how far they would go sexually this evening.

They finished supper while Melissa helped him put away and clean the dishes.

"That was really nummy, and I needed it," Melisa said. "Thanks for help doing dishes," Mick said, "What kind of movie would you like to watch, drama, mystery,..something romantic?"

"Romantic would be good..we are watching them here, right?"

"Yes, I believe I have every movie ever made; we will go back to my bedroom; the room is big, so I have a comfortable couch and a 50 inch TV; I am a movie buff. What would you like to drink, beer or something mixed" Mick said.

"Do you have Corona?" "Yes, I do."

"I will have one of those, and I would like to watch Sleepless in Seattle."

"Sounds good; I will grab a couple of beers, Melisa," he said, "The couch is a little small; we will have to sit close together." She smiled, "No problem."

They both came inside his bedroom with open beers. It was dark, and Mark went over to a bedroom wall where hundreds of movies sat in a huge cabinet. It only took a few seconds until he found the movie she chose. He turned on the TV and cd player, sat down on her left side, picked up the remote, and hit play. It was a minute or two before the movie started playing. They looked at each other, and Mark knew he did not have to wait for anything. They kissed, both put their beer on the small table in front of them, and kissed, not like teenagers, there were no adolescent mockings, they tongued, they knew what they wanted. Mick's right hand went beneath her shirt and was playing with her bra hooks. After detaching them, his hand went up further, grabbed a fistful of hair, and pulled her head back with a quick shrug.

"Oooh...you are a little forceful...a little dominant, I like it," she whispered with her eyes closed, a small grin on her face.

His tongue licked across her neck, he used both hands to take her shirt off, and with the bra detached, it fell on her lap.

She still had her eyes closed, leaned back against the couch. He was licking and sucking on her nipples as her left hand went to his pelvic area to feel the bulge. This lasted for several minutes. The only light in the room was the TV playing a movie. His hand went down to her lumbar area, started rubbing her sexual organs. It was foreplay; the more you have it, the better the sex is.

They both thought we are no longer teenagers, no questions on what they wanted or how they should get it, both 18 and all the inquiries and self-examinations were taken care of years ago; they were not virgins.

Mick thought about himself, "She is a beautiful girl. All she wants is a couple of orgasms, a good time, and get ready for college. I realize that but don't care; what's wrong with me?" He continued foreplay, one hand squeezing breasts and the other rubbing her clitoris. He looked her in the face, as dark as it was with only the TV giving light, eyes closed, and a smile on her face as she leans back into the couch. He thought, "All that stuff I looked up, a bunch of psychological bull shit, or is it real? Homicidal Ideation...it is not a disease but thoughts through primal Delerium of psychosis. He read it may rise in association with personality disorders. Homicidal fantasies are merely a theory, he was no patient, but sometimes he thought he should be. No hallucinations or delusional beliefs, but I always thought of it."

He very lightly grabbed her shoulders and helped her lay on the couch, and her arms went above her head as she softly bit her lower lip, "Hhmmm yes," she whispered. He pulled off her panties and shorts.

He thought, "This almost seems easy..." the question still bothered him, "Am I a looney tune, psychologically insane...or just a guy taking care of fantasies? I have thought about it a thousand times and will in the future. What is it? Insane nutzoid or a feeling, a guy who exactly knows what he is doing?"

He grabbed a rope he had underneath the cushions and pulled it gently across her belly button toward in between her breasts. She looked down and said, "Oh my.....are you getting kinky on me Mick.......ok, be gentle, master." She turned her head sideways and put her hands toward the end of the couch. He tied her arms to the arm couch.

She was lying there naked, arms securely tied to the couch. He played with her breasts and started moving his head toward her vagina. He thought, "Jesus Christ, what the fuck am I? He remembered that killers always say the first murder is always the hardest; the killings afterward are synch. Too late, I can question my thoughts all night long, my movement, my activity is all that matters, what I do, my conscious choice to fulfill my self-realization of what I think I am. My plan must be fulfilled. I will be fulfilled!"

His tongue was licking right by her belly button, and he looked up, eyes closed, licking her lips. He put his left hand beneath the couch cushion, grabbed the hunting knife that used to belong to his father, brought it out and held it with both hands on his knees on the couch, and looked down.

She looked up, and her entire world went 180 degrees in the opposite direction. "Mick," she said, "What are you…….doing," the delightful, enjoyable facial expressions turned to the trepidation of fright and horror.

He never said anything, he never cared, self-inclined of his fulfillment must be done. He stabbed her at the top of her left breast, only in a couple of inches. She shrieked, and as it came out, turned into a scream. His mouth wide open, hands still on the blade's handle, a streak of blood seeped toward her armpit.

At that point, Mick's life turned in the other direction as well. After Melisa's scream came to an end, she started breathing distinctively, loudly. He heard someone in the corner giggle.

The only light in the room was from the TV. It was like light flashing as the movie went on. Mick looked toward the corner and saw eyes as the movie change to different scenes. Mick saw a short man in a three-piece suit and a bowler hat staring at the dreadful, shocking scene.

"Hello…friend," Lucifer said.

"You….have….got….to be fucking kidding," Mick whispered.

"Oh, no, sir, I am quite real," Lucifer stated.

Mick was on top of Melisa's hips, and she was frantically trying to loosen her wrists from the rope, unsuccessful. Mick tries to make a reality of the situation; his victim tied up, a wound to her chest, his first kill, and a……businessman, who somehow entered his house how?

"How the hell did you get in here?" Mick was trying to grapple with the situation, "And who the fuck are you?"

"Like I said before…I am your….friend." Lucifer looked down at Melisa, pulling her hands from the rope, breathing heavily, and near passing out. "I love your work; we must make sure it goes on, in your own way, you must send a message."

Mick was feeling unsteady, lightheaded; he looks at this short man, "Again, who the fuck are you?"

"I am so tired of people asking what's your name," Lucifer said, "I came to learn more about your type of person. What it is you do and why." Lucifer stepped forward and touched Melisa's hair, "Poor Melisa," a dark smile went across his face," You know your first victim, but in the future, your casualties won't know you,..to protect your identity."

This is strange Mick thought, "You were in here for hours, you were in the closet, who the fuck are you?" Melisa was starting to come around; she said, "Mick……please let me go… I won't tell anyone. Let me go…..please, please!" She begged, eyes wide open.

"Well..what are you going to do Mick, let Melisa go call the police because a man broke into your house. What are you going to do?"

Mick thought, "This is not going the way I planned; some freak breaks into my house, just as I am fulfilling my destiny. Kill this guy too, two instead of one."

Mick pulled the knife out of Melisa's chest and sliced the blade squarely across Lucifer's neck, a deep cut leaving a slash end to end. A wound came open, Lucifer's face made no movement. He just stared at Mick, a little smile and a wink. No blood came out, everything inside the slash was black, and it took only seconds to heal. Mick could not find words, and he just gawked at Lucifer.

Melisa simply stared up, mouth wide open, felt like she was going to pass out. Lucifer said, "I will be completely honest with you, Mick; I will forgive you, although I don't know why, of your trying to murder me." He bowed at the waist, "I am the devil."

"Fuck you," Mick stated.

"Think about it, Mick; you slice nearly half my head off, yet here I sit. I could tell you much about the future and past, names, dates… anything you want to hear. Like I said before, I like to learn about your type. And another thing Mick, the reason for my presence is to learn about you; I know quite a bit but police officers refreshing lot to see. If you were…. arrested if you tell police officers you saw the Devil, they would look at each other, they would ask you, what was the Devil wearing, his height, that sort of thing…while they were thinking,…this guy does not need a penitentiary, he needs a loony bin. They would not believe you," Lucifer started to muse himself, giggled again. "They would say nothing to you but think of what you would need is a straight jacket and a white room where you would not hurt yourself. They would feel complete in getting you off the streets..and getting you in a psych ward. I, the Devil, could tell you anything, and no one would believe you."

Mick was at a loss. He did not know what to say or do. Melisa was still breathing heavily, unable to move, staring at the ceiling. The Devil continued, "And that question you keep asking yourself, why am I doing this, it is both a feeling within you and psychologically impaired result. It is both….it is within your surroundings, the way you were raised, and something inside your DNA. You feel it, Mick, it is like a disease, cancer, it grows within you, after poor Melisa is on the slab, you will feel satisfied,.. but weeks will go by, and the unsatisfaction has grown again. You will start looking at different women, a new victim" Lucifer pointed at Mick and chuckled, "You know I am right; once they start, they will never stop."

Mick was wordless, looking at someone who calls himself the Devil. He is right, one massive slice should nearly be taken his head off, yet there he sits. He was right about my self-made cancer; Melisa will be the first of many. He looked up, his eyes looked at the ceiling, "Oh my God," he whimpered, "Really….really.." He looked at the Devil, who was sweetly smiling.

"I have to go run…..errands," Lucifer said, "Start off smartly by burning little Melisa and the couch. It will be full of blood, even after cleaning it. We must make a statement with your actions, and your work must go on repeatedly. Make sure your future victims do not know you. Be smart; keep away from police officers. Our Father is the same, and we must let him know the action of his sons are full of disgrace and shame. He must know…"

Mick looked down at Melisa, slashed the blade across her neck, deep and vicious, looked back up at the Devil, but he was gone. I looked across the entire room at the light of the TV, but he was not there. He thought, "What the fuck just happened, fucking weird!"

He drove her car in the garage and waited until 3 am to burn her and the couch in the backyard fire pit, took the bones and buried them out at his uncle's farm. He had a new…order.

It was dark; it felt like a death in there. Mark B. Anderson was found guilty of 4 homicides; although the detectives and police force agents thought Mark had at least 30 deaths or more in his previous killing spree, the clear proof of the four deaths was all they needed to put him on death row. It had been 17 years since the death of Melisa Christianson that Mark wore his deathly tole. He pleaded not guilty for over ten months until his jurors gave him an impartial verdict of first-degree homicide and a death sentence.

He did not care for the last meal; he gave a braggart response to the guard, "Just gimme a snickers asshole." The only thing he asked for was 15 minutes with Pastor Brown; they gave it to him, at 11:45, 15 minutes before noon, his execution.

The room felt like it was almost faded, dark, baleful, and menacing. Mark was wearing all orange and was handcuffed to the table as Pastor Brown entered the room. He stopped at the door and bowed his head, and prayed whisperingly to himself. He then looked up at Mark; several seconds before he moved forward, he thought he was looking at evil.

"Thank you for a good chat, Pastor," Mick stated.

"God bless you, son," the Pastor sat down on the other end of the table. "Would your soul like to confess my son?"

"My confession really does not mean shit," Mark responded, "It is what it is; I will be stone cold fucking dead in a couple of minutes; it doesn't matter what I confess to." Mark looked at the Pastor for several seconds; you could hear a pin drop. "I would like to ask you a couple of questions. It seems weird."

"What is it, my son?"

"I know this will sound strange….." Mark looked down, hands shackled to the top of the table, "Please have an open mind, Pastor, but when I murdered Melisa, my first victim, something bizarre, something is forbidden something sinister happened" Mark was almost yelling.

"You can trust me what happened," Pastor said.

Mark was breathing hard, "There was…..someone there," Mark shrieked.

Silence for several seconds, Pastor said, "Who?" "After I sliced into her body…I heard a giggle."

"Someone is laughing," the Pastor said.

"Yes…this little guy, in a suit and a bowler hat. His little smile made me sick, with a sharp beard and mustache. He said he was my friend, huh, whatever."

"There was another person there. Did you tell the detectives that?"

"No, I didn't, Pastor." "Why not?"

There was silence. Mark looked at the Pastor, wanted to be sincere, truthful to what he was about to say, wanted the Pastor to believe in him.

Eye to eye Mark finally said, whispering at first, "This guy said he was the devil."

The Pastor's eyes came wide open.

Yelling out loud, "This guy said he was the fucking Devil!"

Silence again, guards outside the door heard Mick, thought, "This guy is really nuts."

"Mick,...you should have told the detectives," Pastor Brown said, "You could have taken a plea and saved your life."

"After my....sinister career, do you think I should be alive" they leered each other, "Pastor Brown...do you believe me that I saw the real principal Satan, as I was liquidating Melisa, I sliced him across the neck, all his peroneal nerves and veins were carved,..but he never bled. It only took half a minute for the wound to heal, fucker winked at me."

Pastor Brown looked back toward the door, did not know what to say, looked back at Mick, mouth open but nothing to say.

Pastor Brown was getting tired of silence, and when no one was talking, it felt like death was right around the corner. Mark said, "The devil said not one god a damned person would believe me...he was right. What you believe is that psychologically, I am telling the truth, I believe it was the devil, but, hahaha, I am insane, but realistically it was a paranoid delusion, no way he was there...right, padre."Mick laughed out loud.

"I feel sorry for you son, you need God's help and love more than ever."

"I hear you, padre, I hear you."

Two guards and a man wearing a suit and a cowboy hat came to the door, 'It's time, Mick."

"Yeah...." Mick stated, "It's time about fucking time, really."

One of the guards unhooked cuffs off the table while the other held a baton if Mick tries anything stupid. Put Mick's hands to his back and cuffed him. All five of them walked to the execution chamber. Pastor Brown opened his bible and started whispering different passages.

As they entered the chamber, two men were there dressed like nurses. One of them opened a curtain to the reporters watching the execution, ugly but necessary. Mick did not want to be judged but had no choice, he gazed at them, and his jaw hit the floor. Among the reporters was a short man in a three-piece suit, a bowler hat with a sharp beard who was winking at him.

Mick howled, shrieked, "Oh God....help me he is right there, don't you see him!"

The sheriff in the cowboy hat said to the guards, "Let us be done with this, hurry up."

As the guards were forcing Mick on the red slab, the other nurse got Mick's arm ready for the needle, the chemical agent that would end his life. In the minute it took them, Mick screamed, "That's him the devil... he is right fucking there....in the other room can't you see him?

Right through the glass right there!"

Mick shifted his head as he was tied to the slab. It looked like one big cross. Mick's mouth and eyes were wide open as he and the Devil stared at each other. That crimson smile from Satan made Mick....insane, mad beyond reason. Not one sane person would ever believe a man with insane acts, killing women, a murderer."OH shit," Mick yelled. "Hurry up, pump that shit in me. Oh god," Mick was shaking, "It's is like that fucker said.....no one would ever believe me the Devil is right there!" Mick leered, glared at the Devil, but no one thought he was sane. The sheriff nodded at the nurse, who hit a button that started the poison from larger containers into Mick's body. As Mick's body was starting to get dizzy as the poison entered, the stare of death, evil, filtered the room. The Devil gave one more wink to Mick as he stared on, an insane look as eyes wide open as the Devil mocked him.

The last thing Mick heard before he went into darkness was Pastor Brown, "God, please help his poor soul."

KILL SHOT
DG

ABRAHAM BEAMONT WAS TIRED OF THE war in front of him, "Damn Germans," he whispered. He felt as though WW1 would be coming to an end soon. He viewed the bunkers, barbed wire, wounded soldiers, trenches for communication and food to starving men. The front he perceived, he judged, had enemies 50 yards away, ingested their own trenches. He was a French Captain in the Ypres Salient for over a year; it was towards the end of October 1918. Edgar, a mere private but Captain Beamont's favorite inferior, crawled up slowly near the captain and gave him a monocular, whispered, "What do you see, Abee"?

"Not much," he whispered back, put the monocular up to his left eye, "I have seen the tops of men's heads moving south in their bunkers. I think they are trying to move heavy stuff, a new canon or chemicals to throw in our face."

"Those fucking bastards," replied Ed, "I would rather be shot than breathe that crap they throw like grenades."

"They are desperate, and they are losing this war and this battle; desperate men would do anything to turn the tide in their favor."

Ed looked at his captain, he knew he was sharp-witted and intelligent when it came to analyzing and scanning the enemy, but in his entire time, Ed never saw Abee kill anything, gave orders; that was pretty much it.

"Abee," said Ed, "We have some more soldiers coming in to end this war, the general and all the upper management think these are the final days for our enemy, we must know to ourselves and them the end will be soon, more backup will let the Germans know that too."

"I see," replied Abee, "I do not want to see more men die. The sooner this is done, the better...when will they be here, have you seen them"?

"A couple of them...there is this one man, short, small, he fires that rifle like no other, never misses."

"Good, I will meet them in the morning, give them orders,... to end this conflict." "Yes, sir."

In the morning, Captain Abee got dressed and came up toward the front line; his bunker was several hundred yards back from the mud and trenches of the killing zone. He met Ed on his way to the front, "Morning, sir," Ed said.

"Morning Ed, I heard some pounding; what am I missing," Abee said as they were walking toward the fronts, kneeling when the foyer lane was not deep enough.

"Germans have a combat vehicle, an iron juggernaut, coming up toward the battle. An airplane saw it was coming about an hour ago; it should be here any minute."

"Oh God, we lost 22 men when the last one attacked. Are the new men here?"

"Yes, they are upfront with the other men."

As they got toward the front bunkers, Abee witnessed something he could not believe, a man, a short man, was standing on the high end of a bunker looking around, almost observing, spectating the battle. Bullets and fragments of erupted blasts all around him.

"You there," Abee screamed, "Get down from there; you could be injured or killed."

The man looked down at Abee, a little smile on his face, looked at Abee for several seconds, replied, "Very well, sir, as you wish." He jumped down, 15 feet high from the bunker, landed with almost no bending of the knee.

Abee looked at Ed, astonished look on his face; they both looked at the man. "I would like to have a word with you later on...if you are still alive, the Germans are sending a killer vehicle towards our side of the battlefield, and we must take it out before it takes us out."

The man still had a little smile on his face, "This machine, this juggernaut, this armored fighting vehicle, is very feared and brings out men's uneasiness, but it has many flaws."

"And those are," Abee said.

"Well,... let's go have a look, and I will show you."

As the men stooped and crawled the eastern end of the trench, they could hear the engine of the first made "tank" get closer; there was a more passable lane or route it was following, the driver did not want to get stuck in a wide trench.

"What is your name," the small man was laying on his stomach, head up, watching the tank get closer; he was right next to Abee.

"Oh, names, there are so many of them."

Anger was hitting Abee, first conclusions. He already hated this little soldier, this little private.

"No, asshole, what is your name?" "Call me Mr. Orcus."

"Ok, Mr. Orcus," Abee let out a laugh, "What are its weaknesses?" Mr. Orcus flipped over on his back, then on his stomach, and had a French Berthier rifle in his hands. "What where did you."

Mr. Orcus giggled, "Heee, ho ho." Aimed the rifle, pulled the trigger.

The German driver of the tank had a narrow casement, an opening about a foot across and an inch and half-open where he could see out, thought to be by its manufacturer to be too small to be a weakness, they were wrong. The driver saw a rifle being fired and half a second later felt a bullet go in between his eyes and out the back of his head. There were four men in the tank. One fired the cannon and machine gun, and another was ready to release chemicals and fire the flame thrower and their lieutenant giving orders. They looked at each other in fear and astonishment as their driver fell dead.

Mr. Orcus grabbed the bolt to put in a new metal jacket into the firing chamber and only a second later fired a new bullet.

The men in the tank were perplexed, surprised, and shocked; they heard another bullet enter the tank, ricochet off a metal wall in the back, and hit the lieutenant in his neck. He went down on his knees and fell down dead. The last two looked at each other, fear-filled them.

Mr. Orcus kept giggling; another bullet fired.

The last two men in the tank had no answers; one slowly put his head through the casement to see out, mistake, the bullet went through his right eye, he fell dead.

Mr. Orcus looked back at Abee and Ed and the soldiers around him, "I am a good shot, don't you think." Put another shell into the firing chamber, pulled the trigger.

The last man in the juggernaut felt fear, didn't move. The bullet ricocheted off a metal fragment and went into his chest.

Abee could see the tank was off course, fell to its side, and just sat there. He had many soldiers around him, "You two, take gas, crawl up to it and start it on fire, you other men, put down a fire barrage to protect them as they start the blaze." "Yes, sir."

Abee had a smile on his face, used his monocular the view the scene. A tank, taken out in minutes, inconceivable. He saw the men gas it quickly, then crawled back; the men around him laid out the fire to protect them. His smile disappeared when he looked at Mr. Orcus, the smile on his face as he looked back at Abee. He remembered psychology many years ago in college, and this man knows something; I can see it in his eyes, just a little private, yet he is mocking me.

"You see, Captain, it has its weaknesses……..everything has its weaknesses, don't you agree?"

Abee looked at this man, thought to himself, "Who the fuck is this guy?"

The next day Abee witnessed a liquidation of manslaughter. The Germans were out to let their nemesis know the battle was far from over. German planes came in as men moved forward to take over their enemies' bunkers. Abee could see the pilots, two in each plane, were throwing grenades and combination bundles of chemicals, throwing them from their arms.

"They are trying to come in from the south," Abee told Ed, "I need to take as many men to the south to be ready for them."

"Yes, sir," Ed said as he ran into the east bunkers to get more men. There were explosions and ricocheting bullets everywhere. Just then, Abee saw what he almost knew was inevitable; Mr. Orcus was right at his side, with rifle ready to go.

"I am ready, sir," Orcus said, "Let us show these Germans what war means; let us show them how to die."

Abee did not know what to say; he would love to hear any other soldier say that, but not him; this private mocks me, I can see it in his eyes.

As Ed came back from other bunkers with men, Abee said, "We need to protect the southern flanks. We will line up and give them hell as they come." As they headed toward the southern bunkers, Abee could see that Mr. Orcus lead the group.

As they got to the southern flanks, the bunkers were not as deep as they should be; men were on their knees or crawling, except Mr. Orcus. Still standing up, he started firing his rifle immediately. Abee pulled out his monocular and observed men moving forward, and each time Mr. Orcus fired, one would fall. The coming soldiers would hide behind extinguished or destroyed cannons, but it would do them no good. A pop from his gun, another man would fall. A German airplane was coming their way. Mr. Orcus aimed his rifle at it pulled the trigger, and the plane quickly fell and exploded. All French soldiers were excited and yelled as they saw this. One yelled, "Keep it up, man......woohoo, keep it up." Another one yelled, "Die german scum die." Abee moved over next to Mr. Orcus, looked at him, "Damn good shot, man." Abee looked through his monocular, "There is still one running back to the German bunkers."

"No problem, sir, no problem," Mr. Orcus said. For a second or two, Abee looked at the running german through his monoculars; for half a second, he wondered how is this possible? He never misses. Better to have him on my side than yours, but still. Right before Mr. Orcus pulled the trigger, Abee did not move except his eye; he looked at Mr. Orcus and felt a quick shock. Mr. Orcus was looking at him. They stared at each other; one-tenth of a second felt like a whole minute.

Abee thought, "You have got to be fucking kidding me."

His rifle went off without Mr. Orcus not seeing the rifle's aim; Abee looked through his monoculars and saw the german fell dead.

Abee and Mr. Orcus looked at each other; Abee thought, "This is beyond reason way too fucking odd." Mr. Orcus smiled.

One day later, Abee was at his tent several hundred meters away from the front, and he sent a private to go get Edgar. He had brought several whiskey bottles, a portion of a captain's gear, brought one out, and poured two glasses half full as Ed just arrived.

"Ed got a nice treat for you, sir." He handed a glass to him. "Thank you, sir."

"There is not much action today, is there Ed? I have heard shots of fire, a few grenades going off."

"No sir," Ed replied, "a plane or two flew over, not much fire from the front." Ed finished off his whiskey in two swallows, "I needed that."

"The reason I called you in Ed...is Mr. Orcus."

"The soldiers love him, think he should be moved up to Lieutenant."

"I.....agree, I just think there is something odd about him.....well... not really odd, his power as a soldier goes beyond reason....to me..." Abee was trying to find the right words, downed his drink, "how can you shoot 100 percent? He never misses. Remember when I asked him his name,... he replied to me, There are so many of them. He said call me Orcus. I looked up what Orcus means," Abee grabbed a book off his desk, "Orcus means the God of the underworld, the broker of oaths."

Ed was starting to have questions about Abee, and he has never seen Abee even hold a gun none the less shoot it. "Sir...Mr. Orcus is on our side; God knows what would happen if he an enemy...you should be thanking him rather than questioning him." Ed had many friends die in this war, and he wanted this war to end. "Why don't we just go ask him" Ed was starting to become angry, "Damn,... maybe you had too much whiskey, sir."

"Do you know where he is at?" "Yes, I do, sir."

Abee and Ed made their way through the bunkers toward the front line. They finally made it to the center-front bunker. Mr. Orcus was talking to other soldiers; they were listening and laughing with Orcus. The soldiers stood as a Captain as the captain arrived.

"Sir."

"At ease," replied Abee. "Mr. Orcus, can we have a word with you?" "Of course, sir."

Abee started walking down the trench toward the south. Ed and Mr. Orcus followed, "Mr. Orcus, where are you from?"

"Oh...Captain Beamont,...I have been all over the world,...let us say...I am from France."

"I would ask you precisely where you are from, but you would not answer me...would you?"

Mr. Orcus smiled, "It seems to me I can be anywhere."

As they stared at each other, they heard a clamor, a tiny sound coming from the German hold. Ed quickly got out his monocular, stood up, and said, "I can see a couple of German soldiers moving; no, it's like they are looking for something." Abee and Ed thought that Mr. Orcus would have his gun out and shoot them as he has always done. Orcus went a couple of feet to his left, where he could see from the trenches better. "Oh, I see them. I don't know what they are doing."

Abee and Ed looked at each other; Mr. Orcus would have them dead in no time; there were two of them, looking around for God knows what.

"Captain Abee," Orcus said, "Why don't you get your first Kill shot?"

Abee said, "What?"

"Cmon, Abee, every soldier knows you have not killed so much as a fly."

"I don't know how much time you have better do it quickly," Ed said as he continued aching the soldiers. Abee felt like a boy; years have gone by why men die at this war. He gave orders, nothing more. Do the soldiers mock me as well? The war has changed our world, and everything will be different; my soldiers and I go home. Will it be the same? I am tired of being a manager. I want to be an eliminator, fight the fight rather than saying how it's done.

"Give me that rifle," Abee hissed at Orcus; he grabbed the rifle and put his arms over the top of the trench, started aiming. The German soldiers were about 40 yards away, pinted on the one sitting a little higher. Mr. Orcus was right by his side, "Breath easily, let your breath out before you pull the trigger." Abee felt like a marksman. He put the rifle's point right on his head. Unmoving perfect. Right before Abee pulled the trigger, Mr. Orcus nudged with his elbow, just a smidge, but enough to change the shot.

"You fucking asshole!"

Mr. Orcus smiled and said, "Oh, I am sorry about that, Abee."

Ed said, "I think you got him in the shoulder," still looking through the monocular. The other German soldier grabbed him and pulled him back in their trench.

"I fucking missed because of you," rages Abee.

"Don't worry, Abee, I can already see you are a killing machine" Mr. Orcus started laughing; the smile on his face enraged Abee. He growled as he went back to his tent to finish the bottle of whiskey. Ed just stood looking at Mr. Orcus, giggling and laughing.

On the German side, toward the back of the German front, a soldier was helping a man into the medical site. The physician quickly helped to put him on the table.

The physician asked, "What happened?"

"A shot," the soldier said, "Hit him in the shoulder; I think he will be ok; the bullet went in and out."

"Let me have a look," the doctor said, "Yeah, there is no bullet, in and out; you are a very lucky man. What is your name?"

The patient, the shot man, stated, "Adolph Adolph Hitler."

The doctor said, "If this bullet were three inches lower, we would be putting you in a casket."

THE PROSECUTOR
Written by Darin Graves

HE FELT HIS MIND EXPAND IN blackness as he pictured the truths of the physical universe reduced to mathematical equations, mind reduced to matter. He sensed a barrier develop between himself and reality; he felt sheathed in its wispy whiteness. Something in his own recent life had gone terribly wrong. Good and Evil whispered to him, well assured him that everything would be alright, "Do good to yourself and others," angelic voices cried out. Evil was guttural and unnatural, "Don't worry," it hissed, "you needn't seek me out; I will find you." The vast blackness was spreading rapidly; it had no edges or shapes but only mass. It was slippery and elusive, and without definition, he felt his mind reel at its infinite reach. He felt he would lose sight of the physical world. He considered the brain and how it dealt with natural reality; how did it make decisions? Did one individual neuron decide what to do, or did it take millions? Was there evil or good neurons to make our choice? It reminded him of some comedy movie with the Devil on one shoulder and an Angel on the other. He imagined spiritual court, and the Devil was the prosecuting attorney.

"All these options that man has, your honor, were not given to him by me, I admit, I improve the longevity and payback of anything from greed to the original sin. The ordinary man is so easily taken." He raised his hands at the judge, "Guilty, your honor." He turned his gaze over to him and squinted his eyes, almost looking ingenious, with some hidden knowledge deep within him, "But I tell you," almost yelling, "While they were still alive just before death approached, these pathetic and almost disembodied people knew where their souls were going. Bill was saying I should not have raped those teenage girls, and Sally told herself I should not have killed my husband for insurance money; Pat thought I should not have killed this girl for jealousy." The Devil looked at the judge, "Hell is the only option." He is right; I am not innocent; he felt thick and claustrophobic fear that something in his life had gone horribly wrong.

The blackness still grew in size; that too increased his fear. He could not believe atomic particles, genes, and chemicals inside the brain could make a man believe to be an atheist. There must be a soul inside of every human being.

He did not need faith to believe in God; he saw proof every time ha saw an act of generosity and kindness, from giving a little boy a quarter so he could buy a pop to scientists finding a cure to cancer. God, in the spiritual court, need not say a thing.

His own barrier was turning into a vacuum; like the blackness, it also increased in size. As a child, his mom often told him, "He is doing it again." She told him he would sit there and not move or speak for about 5 minutes. He was the only one who knew that he was part conscience. His mom had taken him to the hospital earlier, but the doctor told her there was not much he could do. He said it was an absent elongated seizure. He knew that was happening right now. He often thought of it as his own little playground, amazing yet fearful.

He started to think about time, infinite possibilities of things present, and things to be. All that mattered was the all-powerful ever-present now. The future was written on the map of the stars and susceptible to a billion changes or possibilities, or was it? Was there a relationship between space, time, and matter which somehow had all the formulas of the infinite possibilities written into their atomic design? Like the past, did the future have only one possibility? Were the infinite possibilities finite? All these philosophies, some arguably rational, some intuitive, still left him with the problem of evil. He believed that the decay of human moral systems was inclined with the decay of youth.

When children were very young, they will share their skittles. As they grow older, their experience of the world will teach them to keep their own and take what they can. As children grow older, they learn the laws by which our society uses to control, which his grandpa called "the caveman" within every one of us. When an individual breaks laws, he is dealt with by the laws conditional punishment. But if it includes many people, even hundreds or thousands, a mob is united. Knowing that the laws will not keep society in order, knowing that no one will be arrested, the individual does whatever he wants, steal, destroy and even kill.

The blackness was turning grey; he was starting to see the real world again through slitted eyes. He was almost back to reality from his psychological void. His protecting sheath began to sizzle around him like an electrified spider web. He began to see the real world, and he suddenly remembered why something had gone wrong with his life. His awareness was turned into a thinking conscience about five minutes ago; an emotional awareness or change usually caused the seizure. The emotional change was the fact that he just killed one of his best friends ten minutes ago.

Pops of sweat began to grow on his forehead. He was in the master bedroom; he looked down at the bed and was disgusted by what he had done. She was naked and tied down on her stomach, but he could see her face looking up toward the ceiling.

"Oh yeah," he said almost laughingly, "I cut her head off," then started to laugh, which immediately turned into a soft cry.

He looked down in fear at the outrage below him. Something had gone wrong between man and his maker. The proof was on the bed right in front of him. He looked down a little closer; dollops of blackening blood covered the bone-white sheets. Her back and upper buttocks were covered with red stripes where he struck her with his leather belt. He was sickened and disgusted by himself when he saw a magazine folded around and tightened up, sticking out of her anal cavity. Then he looked at the head, eyes half-closed and a stream of blood coming out of the mouth. He remembered how easily the head came off; the meat cleaver he had gotten from the kitchen was lying on the bedroom floor.

The first thing he said to himself was, "Did I really do this?" His Freudian Id spoke back, "Of course, of course, you did it."

"Yes, I did do it," he thought to himself; there was a portion of his mind that tried to defend himself, "I did something socially wrong."

"No," his Id croaked back, "It was murder, cold empty, calculated murder; you brought a loaded gun, did you not?" He looked at his hips, and right underneath his jeans was a loaded .357 pistol. He remembered to bring it with him; if things got out of hand with Angel, he would tell her not to marry Gary. He thought of the Devil again. He wondered if the Devil and Id were the same. The Devil was the prosecuting attorney.

"I invite you to observe, your honor, the man, had murder in his mind before he saw Angel that night," the Devil rumbled quite loudly, "The fact in his tedious and self inclined gesture was not to marry the person of her choice but to marry him. The fact that he came to her place with a loaded weapon on hand goes to show his attitude. Many times she would agree with him to break parts with other boyfriends, that he, for some reason, though they have outlive their usefulness." The Devil looked down, changed his offense.

"She had been his friend for quite a while. He inclined an adult crush on her that she never saw…he thought they were friends and then some." The Devil stopped for a second, looked at him with shining eyes, "The physically never touched; he thought they were lovers though,… He thought she should be marrying him, not Gary…I tell you, your honor, what a sick man!" The Devil chuckled and grinned. "She was going to marry a guy named Gary Hutchinson, for an entire month he thought about nothing else but owned little Angel marrying someone else." The Devil looked like a little boy as he leered and pointed, "Your honor saw what his depraved disgraced capricious anger made him do. The prosecution rests."

He suddenly began to remember coming up to her parent's house, and it was glowing from the sinking sun. He had what he prayed for; Angel was there by herself. Tomorrow she would be marrying Gary.

"Hi Pat, well, tomorrow is the day I will be a happy woman," Angel said in a western way.

"I would like to have a word with you," Pat responded. An unreasoning chill passed through his head; she was a very pretty woman, and the fact she was happy, in a good mood, made his mind freeze in impatience. "Not yet," he hissed to himself; like the flick of a switch, he was amiable. He approached her closely, "Tomorrow is the day, huh?" he said.

"Yes, it is," she said with a smile.

"Do not smile," he thought and then said," I think you should think it over...you have not known him that long...you should know him better... before you indulge in marriage."

She said, "Come on, Pat, you have helped me before with some bad choices I have made, but Gary is not even close to some losers I said yes to before."

He thought she was right; the man she would marry was from a rich family, educated, and treated Angel properly and kindly. Pat was furious; he knew Gary outmatched him, made his eyes boil, internal rage!

She added, "There has to be a guy out there for me; I believe Gary is the one."

"Not me," he snarled out loud; he could be patient no more; they could both see it was instantly getting aggressive. They both could not believe he had said that. "Finally," he thought, "I have told her," in his unsound state, he thought what goodness he had in himself and smiled at her with kindful eyes. She only stared at him, not believing what she heard.

"I love...Gary," she told him.

He looked away, and a thousand thoughts went through his mind in a second. He knew this was his last disappointment in his life. All the years that went by did not give him a counterpart. Frustrated and tormented by his own desires, the girlfriends he had only lasted two weeks at most. He felt immobile for the last month, out of answers for his own questionable life. He quickly thought of his own philosophies in life; no answer there. There was only one philosophy left, better rule in hell than serve in heaven. He saw the Devil smile awkwardly. Time to send the executioner. This was his last fig leaf.

"I am meeting with some friends a bit later, you know where the door is at," Angel said with an upturned jaw.

"She is mocking me," he thought; his love turned to hatred intent. He stood there for a second, only a second. All thoughts were gone; only intense hatred filled every cell in his body. All things negative in his life were because of her. His Id slightly hissed, "because of her."

He was just a second behind her, just a couple of long steps; he was on her grappling her hair. She was turning as she heard him coming, in an aggressive mode rasped. "What are you doing?" waiting for a second, "what the hell are you doing?"

He actually thought of saying something nice to her, something pleasant. But he knew if she was friendly, it would be the thousandth time in his history would repeat itself; his fluctuated personality was too crude for his own future.

She was fighting back as he dragged her into the master bedroom. Her aggression turned defensive as he tugged and ripped her clothes off. "Please, PLEASE," SHE FROWNED out loud. He snarled back.

"I think not." When she was nude, he grabbed the rope he had brought with him.

Devil rumbled out, "Your honor; he brought a rope as well," he opened his arms and said aloud, "I think he knew what he was doing; he came prepared."

He ignored the Devil and went on, tied her stomach down on the bed, and he also ignored her plea to stop.

He knew that bringing this action to an end was lost. He flung out his belt from his pants in a single sweep, "You never thought about myself as a husband? You would say I never told or asked you out for a date or supper or something, but I have! Every time I saw you taken by the limitations of a lesser man, I would tell you of his negative doings. You would agree so much that you were prone to passionate outbursts. I thought you would put the clues together!" As he screamed this to her, the only answer back was screams from her as his belt went forcefully across her buttocks.

All the love and attention to her was gone. All the times they went to movies, had lunch, bowled, did picnics, and went to parties were gone, like a relative died.

He saw several magazines on the floor by the bed, picked one up, and rolled it until it was hard. The belt was not enough; the sadistic within him wanted a real scream. There was not much she could do, and there were no annoying distractions or her calling out for help. There was no one around, and this made him feel he was in charge. He spat on her anus and started pushing the magazine in; his adrenaline made it go in rather easily. He got what he wanted; she screamed to wake the dead. She could only move her body half afoot, not stopping him from pushing the magazine down. This entire episode was happening so quickly; she wanted no more torture. She thought quickly of how to reason with him; she held back the pain. "Why are you doing this Pat, ...why?" She remembered to call him by name, to not treat her like an object. He stopped and looked her in the face, blinked, and looked away.

For him, it was the ultimate question, his own undoing. All the doorways, all the stages he passed through in life, all the masquerades, each time he turned a new corner or found a bit of space between two boulders, it would always, every time, lead him back to the same boring lifestyle. He hated it most of all. Every passage he could find still brought him back to the same chaotic life! His brain, a wasted and pixilated space, had the same unhappy, inglorious, reactionary expression lessened every time!

Angel was thinking about tomorrow, saying yes, the dress, the dance, the family dreams; she hissed, "I hate you," but then thought, "I should not have said that. I do not want him to harm me." She wanted this to end, started thinking about what to say, "I will not press charges, Pat, untie me and leave. We will forget the whole thing, just untie me and leave!"

He saw Devil again; he was not smiling; he looked like a guy on the street corner, said "Too late."

"Yes, too late," he agreed. He remembered the Devil talking about people knew where their souls were going before they died. Rationalistic thinking made him know he might be waiting for his soul, "Damn the Devil!" he thought, "I will see you in hell."

He went to the kitchen and needed something sharp. He looked through many drawers until he found larger meat clever, perfect!

Angel prayed he was leaving, though, "He is leaving, right God? Oh, please make him go far away!" Her prayer was unanswered.

He grappled her hair, holding up her head, and brought his first stroke down incredibly hard. He felt nothing, no emotions, like a machine performing one of its various functions. No emotions encompassing someone's doom. No emotions.

His second strike cut her entire head loose, and he wanted to see the face. When he brought it up, they stared at each other, eye to eye. Then he looked down at the body, its own headless corpse. A second before Angel died, she had a look on her face like she had just gone to a funeral, then a small smile. Death arrived as her expressionless eyes went half shut.

He put her head back on the bed face up, dropped the meat clever on the floor, making blood and spinal fluids spill everywhere. He felt his seizure coming on by the dark impetus look all things had. He was physically jarred to blackness as his memory, in many different directions, half left him in darkness. His mind started to flux in directions unknown. His philosophy, ideas, thoughts to improve, learning, and finally, his last capricious act. Was he a demon? No, just a human being. But he took another human being's life away, destroying her family's hopes and dreams: all gone, his fault. The Devil looked at him, "There will be a pain...over a long period of time," he rasped with a menacing look on his fiery face, his eyes turned bright. "For your um...social distancing," he said mockingly.

Jail time was the last thing he had in mind, I could run, but they will probably catch me, 25 to life? No. He took out his pistol and put the barrel in his mouth. The Devil said one more thing, "You do have guts for a little boy. Is it not sublime that you could be an imp someday. We will see" "There is nothing else I can do," he thought. "Killing her was so easy; it is only afterward doing you feel the pain of destroying dreams and desires. He no longer wanted to think, feel, love, or even dream himself. He had lost it all. I am so sorry, Angel. I hoped you and I would be going to heaven after a long, happy life. It was so dreamy! Sorry, Angel. He pulled the trigger.

ZOONOSIS
June 2019
DG

WUHAN CHINA, 11 MILLION PEOPLE IN the center of China, live their lives every day by going to work. Car industries, multinational companies, and food corporates keep their commercial and economic businesses thriving. Near Guangzhou district where Xinjoa E rd there lies Nanjing market serves exotic animals as food, there is a Hubu alley that has no liability through government or system to protect populations health. The food is cooked and eaten at your discretion.

St. Lucifer was flying on ravens wings, looking down in the night sky as the entire cities area was litten by lights. He discovered a section that was only litten by fire. Drums of wood and bombardments would blaze the entire Hubu alley. He finally found what he was looking for. Zhang Wei came out of his tent, wearing an older tang cloth. He had not worked for several weeks, and it has been two days since he had anything to eat. He was almost used to having things be dire.

Zhang was startled; a bright light came to his eyes but then quickly disappeared. He felt his hair moved, he turned around and there was a man looking at him, but not an ordinary man, he was very short and in a three-piece suit and a bowler hat. He was a bit stunned and alarmed. "Good evening, sir," Lucifer said. "How are you doing on this fine evening?"

Zhang knew only a few words of English. "Who you?" Zhang very slowly opened his arms.

Lucifer replied, "I know what you are thinking; a person dressed like I simply do not belong here, right. Well, I am a businessman. I have several associates in this area of the world. Come to think of it, and I have associates in every portion of this planet. I do not do business where I do not know the quality of its people and area. I demand it," he almost screamed.

Zhang was not feeling good, and it was hard to stand there. He put a hand near his stomach. "Sir, you are very hungry; you need food," Lucifer said, put his hand at his back, and when it came out, it had a bowl of rice. "Eat, sir, eat."

Zhang did not wait; he grabbed the bowl and quickly devoured the bowl in seconds. Lucifer laughed, "Here here...oh haha haaaa, my, you are like a little boy." Zhang ate the entire bowl, looked at Lucifer when the bowl was empty. Lucifer had something he was holding with an outreached hand, his thumb and his first finger held what looked like a pine cone. Zhang looked; further, it was not a cone; it was a bat, its wings were around its little body.

"Sir, you need protein as well, it is very small one swallow, and you are ready to go... heeee...here...it is very nutritious...here heeee."

Zhang did not know what to do, the rice was good and very needed, but he was still hungry.

"Zhang, you know you need it," Lucifer gave a piercing cry.

Zhang quickly snatched the bat, threw it in his mouth, felt it move its wings to escape while he swallowed it whole.

"Heeeeeee....oh my......haaaaaaa." Zhang was terrified, not by swallowing the bat but by the person in front of him; Lucifer cried out, "Go now Zhang, go back to your friends, your relatives, everyone you know and speak to them, spit out jokes and get very close to them, let them know you are still alive!!"

Zhang heard a noise behind him, looked back but saw nothing. When he looked back to this person, this stranger, he was gone, no one there. Zhang did just that. He went to the market and talked to some friends. The raven flew away, "Here..haaaa."

THE MAJESTIC LYRICIST
Written by Darin Graves

DARIN JUST TURNED NINE YEARS OLD in November 1974. He remembered that birthday quite well because it was the first time he had heard a song called Working Man by a band from Canada, called Rush. He was quite young and impressionable; he loved the sound of the singer's voice, so clear, especially the guitar solo. He listened to it again and again and again. He also loved listening to different songs on their as well. Not much on the cover of their first album, but he still liked looking at it...RUSH, a kind of red, dark pink with lines around it, making it was rushing at you.

He remembered looking like a little punk doing his air guitar during Alex Lifeson's guitar on Working Man. He never understood how his life would be mesmerized, puppeteered, almost taken away by a single band. This was their first album; Cleveland was the first city to be fascinated and captivated, almost hypnotized by their musical ability. Coming from Canada, they first had to get a new drummer; John Rutsey had physical problems, they found a man, like no other, and I mean no other, Neil Peart.

As years went by, Darin grew to stay loyal to this band, absolutely loved the lyrics and music they played. These three individuals conversed a band unseen and would never be duplicated. Record after record, they reached perfection; the first time he saw them live was in Bismarck, ND. It was the Signals tour; his admiration for this band grew tenfold, heard one of his favorite songs, Subdivisions. In many of Rush songs, a man can feel it in his soul; Neil Peart has an ability to reach into your mind, no judgment, no felicitation; he understands what you are feeling and with incredible, remarkable, and magnificent words reaches you. Not one human being can do what Neil Peart does, period.

Darin went on with his life, went to NDSU, and received a Bachelor's degree in Psychology in Fargo, ND. Every year, his friends and himself went to Minneapolis to see their band perform their magic. They put so much in every song on each album; Darin looked for bad songs in every album; they were few and far between. He could only imagine the process they used to make flawlessness excellence. It felt, looked, and showed that every song has its own story; he did not care for the bigger immediate mass, they listened to some great bands, but they were not Rush. The fans knew that you either loved them or did not care for them; once a fan, you never go back.

"We all have problems of our own," from Turn the Page from Hold your Fire, Neil had problems that go deep. I will not get into them; like the rest of us, problems are always there.

Each album that came out had its own ora; each song on that album filled the ora. Small or big, each song filled the crusade of the meaning of the album. Neil was so superb and outstanding in combining the messages and passages into each album, flawless.

As the years went by, you were a fan, but you had to lead your life, very much as Geddy said as he became a father. Forty years plus is a long time; as everyone aged, you lived a good life, but you still were a fan. "Time Stand Still" was Neil's way of pointing out time makes prisoners of everyone. See more of the people and the places that surround me now!

The last concert in St. Paul was at the Xcel Energy that I saw was R40 Live Tour. The concert did not start until after 7 pm, and the boys and I were across the street at a bar and grill; we got there at about 3. They were playing as much Rush as humanly possible, and we had lots of food and many alcoholic drinks. The bathrooms were constantly full, and I remember waiting in line. Of course, you are going to be social.

"Hey, I been a fan a long time; how about you?" I almost had to scream to the next guy in line.

"Yeah, they were freaking awesome last night," he replied. "Last night," I responded.

"In Chicago, I will only see them twice this tour," he said. "Shit, I have only seen them 14 times. How many times for you?" "29, I know guys who have seen them over 50."

"God damn, I am a newbie compared to them," I replied. "Once a fan, always a fan!" he yelled.

"Oh...I so much agree!"

I believe that was the best time I have ever seen them; Geddy and Alex looked so calm and collective, professionals! The songs they perpetrate and performed were favorites and are played to perfection. Alex's guitar sounded clear and magnificent. Geddy has still not lost his voice, which I absolutely love.

And the master, king of kings, perched in his golden seat, entertaining everyone, played like no other. I believe that is the thing about Neil Peart; perfection or I will not be apart from it. He is the best drummer on this planet, but what I love about him the best, in his own preeminent way, are, of course, his penmanship, his novelist, his contribution, his ghostwriting, and lyricist! He perceived, detected, identified all feelings and emotions which we take for granted and analyzed them put them to words that went right to our souls. We understood them, and our minds were open to his writings!

Toward the end of 2019, I would spend much time over at my sister's place; 2020 came fast, and toward the end of the first week was a bit odd to me. I woke up at 3:30 am Wednesday the 8th after a peculiar, offbeat dream I had. I was right by a long driveway, tuning guitars, I had one in my hand, and there was a Hercules stand with four more in it at my feet. The driveway was long and curvy, with high bushes on both sides; it was sunny. I heard a car door slam. Neil Peart came walking down the driveway, long hair, like the way he looked for 2112, long mustache. When he got up to me, no words were given. He had a look on his face, almost saying, who are you and why are you here? I took a step back but still close enough to give him the guitar I was holding. He put the strap on his shoulder, smiled, and played a song I never heard before. His style and the passion he engaged in were stunning! I woke up looking at my cell, 3:30 am.

The dream was completely odd because I gave a guitar to a drummer.

I went to have a glass of milk and a cookie and went back to bed.

On Friday, I learned of the death of Neil Peart, I thought about the dream, but it never seemed important at the time. I texted my brother Curt of the heartbreaking news. This was low as it could get; I was unaware of his cancer, I thought I would see him live again. For half an hour, I told myself, "That's life; it will happen to all of us," I tried to be calm. I went to YouTube and watched Peart's drum solos for 3 hours. Drips of tears fell off my chin onto the carpet. I thought for sure I would see him again alive. I am not so absorbing with this news!! Of course, he had a song about it.

Suddenly
You were gone
From all the lives
you left your mark upon

It was not until Saturday I found that he died on January 7th; that is when my dream still did not make sense other than the fact it was the night he died. To me, it was the darkest day of Rock & Roll. Another Neil Peart in the future? No. There is no one who will even come close to him. Geddy and Alex, you are not the only guys who miss him. Darin

CASTLE BRAVO

Written by
Darin Graves

"HEY, DO ANY OF YOU GUYS know who that new guy is?" John C. Clark asked his fellow team.

"No, I have not seen him before, but...given what we are doing now if he is here without being shot by the guards...well, he could be military informant, some portion of the government, or CIA, who knows?," said Brian.

"He is right, John," stated Joseph said, "We would be the last people that would know about anybody if the Marine guards let him live, let's just hope he is not KGB."

The morning of March 1st, 1954, Bikini Atoll was a coral reef in the Marshall Islands consisting of 23 islands surrounding a 230 square mile central lagoon. After WWII, the Atolls inhabitants were relocated in 1946, for which the islands would be a site for America's nuclear tests through 1958. Tests occurred at seven sites in the reef itself, on the sea, in the air, and underwater. The function, military performance was code-named Operation Crossroads.

The lagoon held a "ship graveyard" of boats left from WWII. Castle Bravo was a unique detonation; the first Hydrogen bomb was an experimentation of pure hydrogen metal, fissioning its matter to give out massive amounts of power. John Clark was the managing director of 3 men at a bunker house at the east end of Bikini Atolls island, called Enyu, was his and their orders to enlighten, engage and commence the most massive explosion that mankind has ever seen. Each of them thought this was going this was going to be an average explosion, the scientists and technologists contemplated this would be a five megaton of TNT explosion, mistakes were made, St. Lucifer was the fourth man of their crew, he knew a little bit more than them but kept silent. The lithium deuteride 6 was 40 percent of the emission element for the explosion; the scientists thought that was the only emission able material available on the bomb, By mistake, deuteride 7 was 60 percent of the mass, and scientists thought it would not miss. When the two deuterides combined, the explosion was three times bigger than what they expected. This was more exploring than mankind has ever done, "Father, remember, I did bring materials to humans, uranium, yes, but I never taught them for this," Lucifer thought. "Lessons taught, but will they learn?"

The men were brought up by jeeps across the sand of the beautiful beach, it was a gorgeous morning, and they all admired the scenery, the sun rising across the still water, which leads to the smooth sand. Coconut trees were everywhere; the view was graceful with an elegant panorama. Not a word was given; each man thought, "Why are we doing this? Fish in the ocean, birds here and there, God help us."

They arrived at the bunker, a marine guard spoke up, "We have this little fortress analyzed and put in more concrete around the bottom, steel slabs on the inside and made it hold its own if a tidal wave came along, you should be safe. Most of you were here as we put the equipment and monitors in, and we have strengthened the outside."

John came up to Lucifer, "I am John, the coordinator. Very rarely does the government or military put in extra people so quickly as you, but I don't have much of a choice. Are you from New Mexico, Manhatten Project?"

"I have been there before, love their work," Devil replied. "What is your name?"

"Oh...names, there are so many of them,...all I can say is this, trust me.

I know what I am doing."

John replied, "Ok, if you don't tell me your name, I think upper management does not want me to know; we will keep it at that."

"Good."

The four men got out of jeeps and started walking toward the bunker; the first crew was technicians making sure everything was functional; the four men walked past the three who were making sure everything was in order.

"Are all the instruments functioning, Joe?" John said.

"Yes, after the detonation, look at the Geiger counter, make sure it is in the reasonable level before you come out of the bunker; the matter we are using on this bomb has never been used before...shit can always happen with any experiment." Joe looked at Lucifer, a slight smile on his face, and Joe thought, "Never seen him before; this entire project is getting more experimental and weirder people everywhere; I do not like it."

Before John and his team went inside the bunker, he looked around, color crabs passed by his feet, seagulls and other birds were flying overhead, fish in the sea, his ideas and beliefs, when he was a child, have all been altered—pondering the future? His reasons were out the door. The Devil could read Joe and John's minds, he motioned and thought, "They are only following orders, he giggled, all men should be the same way, they love their lifestyles, a beautiful house, and cabin in some state, good income, wives they want, send the kids to college...yes, all men should be the same... follow orders, kill the earth without knowing it. Earth has cancer...its called humankind! You know I am right, Father."

Joe and John looked at each other, "God help us all."

The Devil cackled and giggled but only had a bijou twinkling grin.

The four men entered the bunker; Brian was the strongest one, so he closed the massive doors, one outside and two more on the inside.

Everything was more science and reasoning as the men checked all instruments. They all assured everything was functioning at its performance.

John could not help it; this new man who joined his team so close to detonation wondered why and thought about this new guy's true mission. So many words about Russian spies, but he knew that Russians caught up to and were surpassing Americans; two Americans were arrested years ago in the Manhatten project, so what else? Why would this short man with a pointed beard be here? The military, CIA, and political men know he is here; I wish I knew. John thought, "This guy could be the devil himself, and the real decision-makers would never let me know."

"Brian and Joseph, how does everything look?"

Brian answered, "Everything's a go; all instruments are positive."

Joseph turned around and gave a thumb up. John looked at Lucifer, "I promised by writing my name on the contract to never question the boss," he took a step toward Lucifer, "But I can not help to wonder why you are here?"

"Why I am here," the Devil told back, from Greek diabolos, Devil means slanderer or accuser, the Devil's favorite hobby leisure activity, his amateur interest is to conceive, many times it is the truth, to conceive men to what they actually believe. He would do just that, tell them the truth and make it seem false.

"Gentlemen, the actual matter, the fission within this incendiary device, is a matter we have never used before," the Devil quoted, "Deuteride, metal hydrogen, has much promise but has never been used, I am here to see its nuclear fallout, radioactive material may be different from other detonations, I begged the bigger bosses to see this blast, this squall upfront, true experience to see what aftermath this blow will give."

Brian and Joseph looked at each other and gave each other a little nod, believing what they heard; John did not buy it.

The Devil smirked inside; two, believe me, one does not, thought to himself, "Oh how I love to divide them."

"Ok, that makes sense, but all I can say is the military commanders should have let me know," John replied. The Devil continued thinking, "I feel sorry for John; he has no clue about who I am and why am I here, he just has to deal with it, I am here, as simple as that."

An hour went by, and Joseph was on the radio making sure all people, boats, and aircraft were out of harm's way when the incendiary, massive blast went off. There was a destroyer 23 miles off toward the east of the detonation, about 3 miles away from Enyu, which will send a helicopter to "rescue" the four men from the bunker. They were the closest ones.

Lucky Dragon #5 was a Japanese fishing boat; there were 23 men on the boat and were 85 miles east, just fishing and making their living. When Castle Bravo ignited, the men saw the sunrise again, perplexed, not knowing what had happened. Three hours later, the men saw snowfall from the sky. The Americans never knew they were there. The snow was nuclear fallout, radioactive sand from Bikini Atoll after the blast went off. The material isotopes were life-threatening. Confused and disoriented from what happened, the men touched the snow, an error, never touch fallout. All of the 23 had exposure and radiation sickness; one died three weeks after exposure.

The four men chattered and gossiped about normal things in everyday life for the next hour, except John. Every once in a while, he would look at Lucifer with questions in his eyes; this experimental event, this phenomenal scenery incident, will expand man's clutch of the world around him. "There is nothing I can do, so quit asking," he thought.

A bell went off; no one said a word; it was aide-memoire that they were 30 minutes away from detonation.

"Joseph, make sure again that all individuals and boats are out of harm's way. Brian checks everything one more time," John stated, looked at Lucifer, never said a word.

Lucifer thought, "It is a little warm in here. I can feel their hairs rising; they don't know what to expect. It is more confusion than uncertainty. They know they must face no hesitation."

The toggle to start the ignition of the deuteride was one button. Actually, the bomb is one uranium atomic explosion that will ignite the deuteride; the atomic explosion crushes the material to the point of fissioning, like a match hitting gasoline. The more gasoline, the bigger the explosion, and their mistake of not knowing deuteride seven will fission as well, metal hydrogen, watch and learn.

Lucifer looked over the situation; the men were doing their jobs, minutes went by as each man took care of his function. The silence was almost deafening. Small bursts of sweat were on every man, lines of sweat down to your chin, uncertainty, and unpredictability.

Lucifer broke the silence, "Who is going to hit the button?"

"I am," answered John, "Unless you were told you could do it" John was losing his cool, sweating, was not thinking properly, was tired of being the military's puppet. "Why don't you just hit the button? It does not really matter who hits it, just as long as someone does it."

Lucifer likes to set the stage, sets it in motion, and lets someone else do the sin, "Brian, why don't you ignite it?"

Brian looked over his shoulder, "Ok...I will snatch it."

It was getting close to ground zero; John did not like the situation at all; he had a little bit more of the bomb they were detonating than Brian and Joseph and that short oddity that just plain showed up. Uncertainty and precariousness were in true command of this entire operation, true experimentation.

"We are down to minutes," Brian said, "All the precautionary tables have been measured. All systems go."

One minute on the system clock, each man felt pressure, wound up like toys. They knew yet did not know what was going to happen. Brian had his finger on the button, and Joseph had a hand clock, ready to let them know after blast how long the convulsion and tremors would arrive after analysis, shock wave after the blast. Lucifer was calm, peaceful in a way.

When the clock hit zero, John pointed at Brian, "God help us." Lucifer grinned. Brian hit the button, after that, Joseph started his watch, watching the seconds. Electricity fired through the cable, which was 22 miles long back to ground zero. Joseph started counting, 2 seconds at a time, "2...4...6...8...they looked at each other, there was no stopping this! When Joseph got to 20, he stopped counting, hit like a massive earthquake, the walls creaked and shook like they were made of styrofoam. The resonation of the blast was loud and discreet as the southwest wall corner was coming apart like it was separating. All equipment was shaking. The vibration from the floor made it hard to stand. For the men, there was nothing to say. The burning metal hydrogen lasted 90 seconds as the mushroom cloud would rise. An airblast hit them. After 50 seconds after detonation, everything was still shuddering and vibrating. It went on past 90 seconds.

"John, should it be this long? I mean shit..." Joseph said.

John replied, "No, it should have been 40 to 50 seconds...something is wrong."

Lucifer was calm, but no one really noticed. 2 minutes went by when everything returned to what seems to be normal.

"Brian, go out and see how things look," John said.

"Uhm...ok," he responded. Heading out the inner door to get to the outdoor.

John grabbed the wireless radio, which connected them with the destroyer," This is Enyu 1, send in the helicopter, right away!," then looked at Lucifer, "Well, what do you think?"

"There are many men who have done their jobs, and I take off my hat to them," he replied.

The commander on the destroyer called out, "Enyu 1, it will be there in 5 minutes."

John and Joseph looked at each other, "Nuclear fallout shit, do we have any protective gear or clothing?"

Brian answered, "No, they simply thought that we would not need it; at a five megaton, we would not need it."

"God damn it," John screamed.

"More shit news," Joseph said, "Look at the Geiger counter" John and Brian looked at it.

The Geiger counter was at 150 counts per second; 20 or below is ok; it was at 150 and rising.

John was to the limits. He held his head and whispered to himself, "Be calm, think."

Lucifer was enjoying himself, watching men try to engage the position, caught in a trap which they made themselves, too sublime!

John said, "Follow me." he went out the south door and went down a couple of yards to a room which had beds in it, "The chopper will be here in 3 minutes, everybody grabs a sheet," pulled out his knife, "Cut a place for your eyes to see out, being close to fallout is bad enough, you cannot let it touch your flesh." They all knew he was right.

Lucifer was laughing to himself, "Yay, it's Halloween," he thought. "Brian, how far is it to the landing pad," John asked.

"About 100 yards are going toward the beach," Brian replied.

They all got to the last door, listened. "There, the helicopter is coming in," John said.

The door was opened, it looked bright outdoors, they could see the sun as a circle as the nuclear fallout shaded its bright glow. 4 men underneath white sheets came jogging out toward the landing helicopter, as the copter was landing, it was sending nuclear debris everywhere.

"Oh, shit," John screamed. As they started getting aboard the helicopter, there were only 3 of them; John looked back toward the bunker, saw a sheet lying on the ground and what he believes is a Raven flying away. "I am not going to miss you."

A military boat 2016, radioactive levels for Bikini Atoll are 639 mrem yr-1, well above the standard safety for habitation, probably for over 100 years, the Raven smiles.

TRAPPER'S PURGATORY

Written by
Darin Graves

SABASTIAN ELSTAD HAD A TOUGH, RUGGED day ahead of him, but he was resilient and determined, rowdy and unruly he was in his own way. His grandfather farmed and plowed this soil and silt for a hundred years ahead of him. Raising livestock and growing crops was his lifeline, he thought many times, this is it, farming, I could not do anything but farm!

Farming was not an easy task; the work is relentless, you have to get things done according to very specific timetables and fill in what needs to be done in between. His family and family before him farmed this earth, this sod, this mold in southeast North Dakota for generations. Sebastian, called Sabby from his older brother, loved the land and the lifestyle God had given him. He loved his family and all the other farmers in his counties. He was a fairly easy person to live with, but like anyone else, he has mental flaws, individual flaws.

Sabby loves to trap. When Sabby was a little boy, he learned from his dad how to properly trap; there are several laws that prohibit cruel or unmarked ways of treating trapped animals within a trap when they are still alive. To trap these days, you have to be licensed; Sabby is not. What God-given right has the state to make me be licensed for something on my land done by me? The use of any exposed bait or visible attractors is not permitted by law; no trap during the close season. Traps have to be in a proper place and removed when the season comes to an end. All trap laws were disobeyed by Sabby. He uses Duke Coil foothold traps any time any place anywhere he sees fit, held securely to the ground so the animal could not run away.

As a boy, Sabby was doing his chores on the farm when he heard a noise coming from the river, an animal crying in pain. As he approached, he saw his own dog, six months old, was in a trap as he howled and pulled, trying to free itself from hell.

"Oh my God," he shrieked as he went down by the water's edge to help his dog. The dog was friendly at first, licked Sabby's face, and let out some whimpers and moans as his front paw was bleeding, held by a vicious, ruthless maw!

"Hold on, Buddy, I will get this thing off you," the trap was on firmly and was giving no coil to be removed. It held with no remorse! As he was struggling with the trap, the jaws moved a smidgen, not coming off but still causing more pain in Buddy. The dog let out a howl and, by natural physiological past, tried to protect and guard itself; the dog bit into Sabby arm, giving him a brutal bite drawing blood.

"Oww...oh God," Sabby screamed as they let go of the dog and jogged up the bank and into the field; they looked back at each other, this was a massive changing point in Sabby's life, a critical time, tension, stress, and anxiety of decisions to be made.

He whispered to himself, "My dog bit me," it altered the way he grew up. His human life cycle altered that moment; from that point on, he would trap whatever, however, and whenever he wanted to. Another law is that an animal is trapped; there is a 24-hour limit to ease its pain of being held. Throughout the years, Sabby saw hundreds of animals trapped. He let them live, came back after death, they might bite me.

Years went by for trapping while he farmed a thousand acres, dozens of years ago, trapping cougars and wolves was common, but those creatures are very scarce in this soil, more west and south. Rabbits, foxes, raccoons, beavers, squirrels, dogs, and coyotes were common simply from the bait of cabbage, marshmallows, cantaloupe, peanuts, and canned fish. Sabby did not care for the law; he was trapped where ever he felt the need. He has developed the ability to make "gin traps," placing the bait in a position to get the neck, Sabby, just for spite's sake, positioned it to get a leg, then let time kill its prey, not quickly.

Years went by, Sabby loved his normal life, simple yet hard work farming, his favorite holiday was Thanksgiving. He just turned 80 years old but always kept in good shape to run the tractor. Sabby almost starved himself before Thanksgiving, enjoyed eating home-cooked meals with food grown on his own farm, potatoes, green peas, turkey, pumpkins for pie and carrots, and homemade gravy.

"Tomorrow is Thanksgiving, oh am I am looking forward to it!," he was getting all the food collected for his wife to cook. He was singing along, reached down to pick up potatoes when he felt numbness in his left hand. Stopped singing; it felt intense. It moved along up to his shoulder.

"No, no," he whispered; he knew something was wrong. Acute and severe fervid pain went through his chest. He could sense his primal organs were malfunctioning, fell to his knees, sat there for a second, "Oh God," could feel Mudd hitting his face as he went limpid.

Everything was bright, beautiful day in a field much like his own on the farm, not too far from the river. Everything was green, the trees, and the tall grass, bushes, and shrubs; it looked like spring. He glanced around, a gorgeous day; the sun was shining, and the river's water moved so quickly. A great day except for one thing, he was starving—discomfort from the ache of an empty tummy, not good for Sabby.

"Where am I....is this my farm, it looks that way, but it is still a little off." The abnormal look or touch was disturbing, it looks like my place, but the odd parallel had him confused, "And the hunger, I could eat a whole turkey right now, damn I am hungry." The ravenous feel was disturbing.

He looked all around; every single thing was the same but still altered; the distance had a glow and was bright, shaky, and dizzy when I look into it. He saw something move to his right, a wolf? They came and disappeared in a heartbeat.

He shook his head, "Where am I?" another movement to his left, "God damn it," he saw a fox jogging quickly by. Everything looked rearranged and disorganized; he was light-headed as he axiom the environment and horizon. This looks like the farm, but no, and the hunger I feel is killing me.

His hair stood up on his neck, felt something, turned around, and someone was there.

Lucifer was dressed as a French chef, a toque Blanche cookers hat on his head and a white robe, "Oh Sabby, I had to meet you," he said, stood there with a plate of Thanksgiving food on it, turkey breast, mashed potatoes, greens, and carrots, was eating small bits in front of a starving soul.

"This food is so good, much like the bait you put in and around your traps, right Sabby?"

Sabastian did not know what to think; he remembered his heart attack, then showing up in some field looking like his farm but distorted, then a short chef with a pointy mustache and eating food while I starve.

"Yes, Sabby, I had to meet the man who causes much pain...then walks away," Lucifer said. "You are my kind of person."

Sabby saw everything go against his favor, he did not know this was hell, but he knew it was not heaven. "I am his kind of person," Sabby thought to himself," he has to be talking about regarding my years of trapping animals; yes, I left them to die."

Lucifer read his mind, "Yes, Sabby, hundreds if not thousands of cruelty trapped animals you trapped and left to die, not one animal did you put out of its misery, you came back later to dead carcasses, yes Sabby, you are my kind of person,...oh the delightful pain."

Sabby was coming to realize he was in no position to barter; he thought he had a heart attack...then suddenly here, where everything looked warped, abnormal and depraved, almost perverted when he looks into the horizon, and oh so hungry!

"If you are talking about my trapping,...I believe it is my right; I pay my taxes..it is my land, my God-given right to do so as I see fit," Sabby stated.

Lucifer laughed out loud, no chuckle, cackled for almost a minute, "God-given right...yes Sabby, God loves it when a fox is trying to feed its pups, dies under your coiled traps, coyotes, raccoons, all kinds of animals die, by your hands, God would love to meet you."

Sabby and the devil looked at each other; several seconds went by, "Sir...I noticed that you have a plate full of delicious food...I am rather starving...could I have some?" Sabby politely asked.

The devil gazed at Sabby, almost focused, said, "Sabby, you do not need to ask for food; look over there."

Sabby looked across the grassy field; he saw a sign, nothing holding it up, just sitting above the ground about 30 yards away that said, "ALL YOU CAN EAT."

Sabby whispered to himself, "I am so hungry."

Lucifer screamed, "Go forth, my friend, all you can eat is meat and poultry...vegetables...grains beans and nuts....fruits...fish and seafood. American type foods: hamburgers and hotdogs, French fries, pizza, you name it, we got it! Your favorite, turkey and mashed potatoes, pies and desserts, wash it down with a cold drink or a nice German beer anything!"

Sabby gazed toward the sign again; this time, there were steaming buffets of food; between them were tables of plates that held fried chicken, hamburgers, pies, noodles, and pizza beneath the sign. "Time to eat," Sabby said, looked back at Lucifer, but he was gone.

The hunger inside was almost a true pain; he started walking towards the buffet. It was about 30 yards away, the smell, the look of plates of food, delectable, mouthwatering, tasty, appetizing, delicious food! "I am so hungry."

As he was walking toward the buffet, behind him, a snap, he stopped, look behind him. Saw nothing, continued moving forward to the canteen smorgasbord. He was almost there when he heard a louder, roaring snap, looked behind and he saw it, a bear trap! From its hinges came flying off the ground, needle-sharp teeth snapping together as they flew through the air.

"Oh shit," he whispered; the distorted place he was in was looking grim; everything he saw here was distorted, it looked like his farm, but everything was twisted, warped, and deviant. He had a hard time telling distance; is that 100 yards away or 100 miles away? The animals that I saw before are there more of them watching me? I am so very hungry. He had no choice, continued walking for the food, looking down at the ground for hidden traps. Almost there, ten more feet.

He was ready to take a step forward when he heard a snarl; he slowly looked back over the ground he just walked across, a coyote growling at him, "Oh crap," he smuggled, the earth, the terra firma he walked over had traps everywhere, small, big and medium, spring-powered steel-jaw traps, some of which are banned in different countries. Hundreds of them crowded across the field; he looked back at the food and felt the pain of hunger, took one step, and felt incredible pain on his left leg like half his leg was being bitten off.

Fell to the ground, his lower leg in a bear maw trap, screamed in pain, "I know now," he whispered as he finally got threw howling in suffered agony, "This is not heaven its hell," the many plates of fried chicken, pizza, meatballs, and shrimp were within a foot or two from him grabbing. The torment and suffering from the trap were almost as bad as the hunger pains; his smell was intact, a torment of everything ambrosial fragrant tasting so good!

He was there for hours, the jaws of the trap biting past flesh and going into bone; he tried to take it off, reminded him of the dog he tried to help when he was a boy, but the mandible, the jawbone of the trap was not giving, it bit harder every time he tried to remove it.

"Oh God, help me," every time he looked around hell, he could see animals looking at him and mocking him, from squirrels to wolves, from rabbits to bobcats, gaping and focusing on his suffering as they looked and walked away.

Hours went by, failure in trying the take off the trap, more pain, he could hear wolves cry in the distance. The hunger was astonishingly painful, the food was not getting old, the aroma, the scent of the nourishment was mouthwateringly driven to him to move forward and grab it, but the chain of the trap would not give him an inch. Torture and torment!

"This is agony," he yelled; the hunger felt like an empty hole, extreme heartburn as the starvation simply grows, "This is fucking Hell!" Scrumptious food inches away from his grasp, he felt like his lower leg fell off, he stared at it every now and again, his blood everywhere and the spring continued to add pressure, felt like it would go through the bones any time. Suffering brought out humility in his soul, "Over the years I have done this to a thousand animals, never had mercy at the time did not think I had to. I looked about life in an ugly way, the pain those creatures felt had it coming…wrong, I know that now…now I am feeling what they were feeling…maybe I should suffer he could hear the wolves howl in the distance, how long will I be here?

THE CHOICE

Written by Darin Graves

CHAD WAS SLOWLY WAKING UP INSIDE the warehouse, moderately he regained his conscientiousness. Dark and dreary, it felt in there; it was a minute cool in there. He looked around, saw a man smoking a cigarette looking down at him. Then it suddenly hit him, he was in serious trouble, like he was hit on the head, his imperceptible memory slowly threw his headache. He thought to himself, "God, I have made so many fucking mistakes."

He looked around the pitch dark, cataclysmic depository as best he could; no doors or exists he could see. He was in a chair, arms tied and taped the armchairs.

The Devil was higher up on the second floor, looking down on occasion. "What is the difference between a serial killer and a killer? Hmm... the killer is more business type; he only kills when he has to...3 kills in one week...one kill every five years...only when it's needed. The serial killer has a need, psychologically. He feels the presence within him to release the pressure, he kills and feels fantastic...but the weeks and months go by, and he feels the pressure once again, so, kills again, it goes on and on..."

"Hey, Chad," the man with the cigarette said, "You have been sitting there for almost two hours, ready to splash some water on you and say wake the fuck up." Chad looked up at him but could not recognize him. "Do you know who I am?"

Chad looked at him for several moments, "No..."

"You have probably heard of me; I am Axel, the man who does Mr. Schmidt's dirty work." Chad had never seen him but knew who he was; Chad owed Mr. Schmidt money, all would be forgiven if he murdered an enemy of Mr. Schmidts, but when he saw it was a 17-year-old girl, Chad couldn't do it; she was a daughter of a Bank owner. Mr. Schmidt has no pity, kill you and your family.

"I have some bad news for you, Chad; you are tied up in this warehouse; when you leave, it will be in a body bag or several cardboard boxes. Tell all the Angels and Saints you never had a choice, and even they could not save you."

The Devil gave a grin from ear to ear. "I...could not kill a girl," Chad said.

"Oh... that's right," Axel said, "Couldn't eliminate a little girl... that's your problem, you have to be a wolf, which it does not matter, that the boss wants them dead does." Axel bent at the knees and looked into Chad's eyes, yelled," You did not know what Mr. Schmidt does; you are a fucking moron when you knew the business, when billions of dollars are involved do the deed or give the Devil his due." The Devil was enjoying himself.

"As I said before, an associate of mine has been watching you, you were given the information of what needed to be done," Axel said, "But never did it, you were talking to a person we did not recognize was he an officer...a police officer?"

Chad realized the less they know them better; he was FBI, "What guy, what are you talking about?"

Axel stopped, looked at Chad for several seconds, never moved, eye to eye. "You are a fucking liar; I can see it in your eyes." Axel had his hands on his knees, looking at Chad a foot away from him. "Fucking...god damned liar." Axel took a few steps back. "What we have here is an associate, who won't do what he is told to do. That little girl you were going to kill would have been a message to his father and friends, telling them, our orders will be followed, like the Russian mob, we will kill you...and your family. You never carried out your orders,..which is why we are here."

Axel walked over next to the chair Chad was tied in, a little counter, a work surface full of medical equipment, including cutting and incising instruments, slicing surgical tools, and several needles full of fluids.

"Chad, I have been around the block with my career; you talked to a person we have not yet identified, in the last 48 hours, you disobeyed orders, made contact with someone we are unaware of, and tried to run like a teeny mouse, but I found you...so here we stand. I am not here to ask you questions, and I am here to eliminate you."

The Devil thought, "These roundabout killers are omnipresent, here and there, everywhere."

Axel bent down and pulled out a camera that stood on a three-legged stand. "I am going to make a message by tormenting your body; the film, of course, will be sent to Mr. Shmidt's foes."

Chad was perspiring, felt nauseous. Looking at the instruments on the counter, hoping they would not be used on him, "I have money..."

Axel started to chortle and chuckle, "Ha...really fucker...got a billion or two? Ha..what mini amount of cash you have means nothing to me. I am loyal to Mr. Shmidt. Believe it or not, he is like a father to me."

"Loyalty, that is a hard thing to find these days," the Devil thought. "Listen, asshole; I have a daughter myself," Axel stated, "I could have killed that girl, but you couldn't, that I understand. Too many rabbits among the wolves, I am going to cut off every finger and cauterize each wound with a blow torch to make sure you would not lose too much blood, all on tape. I would have given you a sort of cholesterol drug, an anti aspirin which makes your nerves and cells feel additional pain. All of this on a nice CD I was going to call, Obey the Orders."

"Please... no, you don't have to," Chad pleaded and thought, "The FBI guy can't even remember his name. He knew the car I was driving. Is there any chance he followed me, just like Axel did?"

"You know...I can't believe I am doing this, but I will give you a choice," Axel stated.

"A choice?" Chad said.

"Yes, a choice; I will take my 9mm and blow your head off right now, you will take that or long slow torture for several hours or maybe a day," Axel said.

"How would that help me?" Chad asked.

"We are in a downtown warehouse on the weekend; ultimately, someone will be here, it's a matter of time, but someone will come through the doors. If I slowly....torment you... a person or two will be here. Maybe that cop you were talking to, who knows?"

Chad said, "That is a small window; not much of a chance that will happen."

"I agree," said Axel.

"Is there any way you could let me get away" Chad pleaded.

"No, if that happens, I will be the one getting my fingers cut off. The first thing is to never fuck with the boss. If you were smart, you would take a bullet in the brain; I have done this before, a couple of hours of abuse and torment,...slicing things...off, you would ultimately be asking for death."

"He is so experienced," the Devil thought.

Chad looked up towards the ceiling, "Oh God, please help me. "God... any God is not here today," Axel said.

"Oh, he is so right," the Devil agreed. Just then, the Devil saw a shadow move by one of the giant windows, a second shadow? "This is a strange, bizarre event, and the tables are turning for our little mice Chad."

"What will it be, asshole," Axel said, "A bullet or torture?"

Suddenly, two larger chamber doors came flying open on the corner of the warehouse, "FBI, stop what you are doing," the agent blaringly screamed out loud.

Axel immediately went for his 9mm from his belt, turned going down to the floor, and brought his firearm to bear on the agents, and it did him no good. Shots were fired from the two FBI agents, and Chad could see from his point of view that Axel was struck many times by oncoming bullets. Axel's gun fell several feet away from him. The two agents, holding their guns with both hands, came jogging forth. Axel moved forward, tried to grab his pistol.

"Do not go for the gun," the agent howled out very loud. He did anyway.

The agents opened fire again. Axel's life was gone. Chad's mouth was wide open, ready to pass out. The Devil turned into a raven and was headed for the doors, thought to himself, "Sometimes the odd number wins."

ETHICS?

Written by Darin Graves

"AH, THERE IT IS," THE DEVIL thought to himself, "This should be very, very interesting." As a raven, he flew down to the Chicago building. He was aware of a meeting that would take place with men who were leaders in their financial and political fields, not all America but global. It was the year 1923, and different countries had a golden opportunity, but only to themselves, not the masses. Back in June 1903, the Ford corporation made a living in America in an industrial way, better for harvesting and traveling. Soon the oil boom would be starting. WWI came to a close, and leaders of the world would be able to see how financial gains were starting and establishing. They were not there to establish how it would help their countries but how a combination of the leaders would be able to control the world. There was a person named John Nelson Darby, who was a Christian eschatologist who predicted a global conspiracy to impose a tyrannical New World Order governing structures as the fulfillment of prophecies about the end of time. Many of the men here were aware of him but knew no one took him seriously; he was way too biblical.

The Devil landed and looked into a window as a mirror to make sure his bowler hat was on properly. It was 1923 at the Edgewater Beach Hotel in Chicago, the meeting place for establishing and institute order for leaders of the world, not the people.

Arthur Cotton, the leader of land and agriculture, was there; St. Lucifer was hidden at the back of a gorgeous bar-lined room; prohibition was in effect for most of America, not all. The room had neon-lighted bars full of liquors and intoxicants; you could have whatever you wanted. Henry Ford and several of his family were there. Leon Fraser, president of the Bank of International, was there. Howard Hopson was the president of the biggest oil and gas company. Ivan Krueger had the greatest land and housing monopoly, Charles Swan was in charge of the biggest steel company. The men with the most important news were Richard Whitney and Jesse Livermore, and they guided the New York stock exchange to the creation of greed at Wall Street. The Devil's exhilaration and enthusiasm were on high expectations, God's beautiful creatures! These piglets! Taking advantage of what the Father gave them! Their cruel greed will grasp them, and the Devil knew many of these charming and delightful creatures would ultimately commit suicide or lose their minds in an insane asylum. "Fingers of righteousness will strangle them all," the Devil thought.

Arthur, Charles, and Howard were finishing up their drinks, already feeling the buzz.

Howard said, "Did you guys see that short guy...in the suit and hat, who is he?"

Charles replied, "Yeah, I saw him; it looks like he is from Europe or something, glancing around...just looking, I have not seen him talk to anyone yet."

Arthur stated, "Some of the articles we are going to discuss this day. I hope he is not a Judge."

Howard said, "Hey... it's about to start, those New York Wall Street guys ready to speak."

Ricard Whitney and Jesse Livermore came up to the front table. Richard stated, "Good evening, Gentlemen. I hope you all had an easy trip to Chicago. You are here for a great time, making sure you get what entertains you and enlighten you to a new horizon."

Jesse stated, "When we look at the country and the globe, there is huge, massive information of a new world in front of us, there were certain generals who thought it would be unwise to use airplanes in WWI, they were wrong, now those airplanes will be used for traveling. Mr. Ford has made a corporation to build cars, again good for more traveling. I hope you can see what this new world offers. The future is wide open, and there will be tons of cash to be made from this, traveling for business, curious probing, and entertainment. Howard Hopson will feed these machines, oil to gas, and make them standard. The future is wide open, and we can control everything...food, business, traveling, housing, gas, and oil, medical and yes, entertainment, and ah, don't forget political."

Howard continued, "We want everything to be in mass, small is for suckers, across America and the globe, we sell in bulk. We are going to change life for everybody, most people will love this, and we will become millionaires."

Jesse said, "Howard and I work in New York; we sell money, stocks, and bonds. As each of these new products will maintain substance and power, your large amounts of cash will grow even more. As time goes by, stocks will fall but mostly rise. Inside information, we will all ascertain and determine the best ones to buy."

Howard added, "The timing is perfect; we can analyze and inspect what will be good for this countries future, thus buy what's best. A drink!!" The Devil, hidden in the corner of the room, had a fervor, enthusiastic smile on his face. He thought should I enjoy this or not... Yes, I should appreciate it now...tear their souls to pieces later. Oh Father, are you watching this,... God's beautiful creatures!

All the men raised their drinks and screamed, "Success!!" Everyone downed their drinks.

Howard continued, "One thing everyone in this room,...must bear their loyalty to our new clique, our new gang,...our new order. There are certain parties who will make sure our future meetings will be kept, from different times, you will not know about them until a time and place have been sought. When you leave this room, you will never tell what happened here, and loyalty must be 100 percent."

Jesse added," power and money will fill your family, but only to those who are Loyal. If you....disobey these orders,...you will be eliminated."

Howard pulled up a box that was sitting on the floor and put it on the table, opened its lock, and pulled out a human skull.

"Oh, these clever little piglets," the Devil thought, "They think of everything."

Howard said, "This person's name does not matter....the fact he disobeyed does."

Jesse said, "All of you shall come up here and touch the skull and pronounce your loyalty."

All of them did just that.

Each of them came forward and submitted their lives and loyalty to the clique. All doors were shut, only the member's aphorism, their motto had epigram to complete devotion and allegiance to their clique, new world order.

When all was complete, there was a moment of silence. Each man looked at each other with questions, what just occurred? A stream of confusion went through some men's minds; advantageous, content, and jovial went through others; you could tell that by their little smiles. Most of them were favorable.

"Oh, Father," the Devil thought, "This is the real beginning of human's true nature...oh those little piglets." He could not help it, started to chuckle, cackled, and started clapping; the rest of the men looked back at the Devil.

Arthur whispered to Charles, "It's that European guy; I think he wants to be a millionaire too."

Charles said with a smile on his face, "Yeah, he looks the part; we will all be millionaires." All men started clapping, everyone looked back to the front of the room, Jesse opened the large front door, numerous women, dressed only in lingerie, came dancing in the room.

Jesse stated, "These women are willing and able to amuse, please, delight, and charm their master's pleasures. Enjoy!!"

The Devil had a disfigured twinkle on his face; he thought, "How sublime."

There had been many meetings since the first one, boring mostly, same as the first, Howard Hopson was not loyal to the clique, they did not kill him, they put him in an insane asylum where no one would listen to his pleas. The clique does not show pity.

"I have a sense...that this one will be a little different," the Devil thought. It was June 1941; the world was watching WWII was putting the globe into a headlock. Countries had questions to answer, join, or stand aside. US population was against the war, let them kill each other, we are on the other side of the planet.

The meeting was in a bunker in San Diego, southwest just above Mexico, fully locked as men were waiting for good news. There were more men every year, a dozen when the clique started this charade, now 40 or 50 of them, leaders who wanted to control and dominate the world. The Devil thought, "These little mice, control now, Hell later."

Orvil Anderson, many year generals, went to the table in front, "Good evening gentlemen, I hope all of you are moving forward, Financial and informational. Our order has given us inside information to make our lives tranquil and serene in controlling all around us." He looked down, blinked his eyes, "I will be clear and won't take up much of your time; the war is...rejected and declined by the US residents. The citizenry does not want it. We have to think in a different way. Financially we can not afford to NOT join the war. Billions of dollars would be put into the construction of military hardware; planes would be bigger, boats and aircraft carriers, tanks, and jeeps. Rifles and simple articles for soldiers. It would be massive, and gentlemen, I know what you are thinking, you already know as much as I do, your children will go to college, the lesser man's son will die... it's as simple as that."

"Oh, you little piglets," thought the Devil, "My demons are going to enjoy your purgatory."

A voice cried out, "The population does not want to go to war; how can that be switched?"

Orvil replied, "We have given that considerable thought," the general looked at a captain standing next to him; they both nodded at each other, the general looked back at the men, "We need to be...hit by an enemy nation, all people will change their minds when we, the United States becomes the victim." People started whispering.

The general took a big breath, held his head high, "Japan has many different areas to attack us. After they hit, the population will want, and I mean, want war."

"Father...are you watching this" the Devil twinkled.

All the men started whispering, and a younger man whispered, "That makes sense."

Orvil continued, "The naval sources, all their ships move consistently, but the Pacific ocean is massive, there are many places we will keep open, to attack. Hopefully, it will be soon; a company named Boeing has elite construction for bombers. Essex carriers will be moving tons of material to our front. Like I said before, the United States cannot afford not to be in this war. Billions of dollars gentlemen, as the money flows, it will ultimately end up in our pockets."

"Money is the root of all evil, is it not Father?" Devil whispered.

The captain next to Orvil put a bag on the table in front of them; Orvil pulled out the skull and held it high on his left hand, yelled out, "I received this skull from Paris, France, all I was told he is high in the clique. Everyone here must touch it and give loyal, absolutely loyal treatment to our brotherhood. Betrayal will not be tolerated. Touch it and give your submission."

All men in the room did it. The Devil came out of his crawl space in the back and moved up front toward the general and the captain. Many of the men in the bunker were wearing military uniforms with several in 3 piece suits; the Devil walked right up to the general and asked, "General sir, I received some information about. a new weapon, a different weapon."

The general did the same thing he always does; look at the captain, they nodded. "Yes, we received direct details from London, as a matter of keeping them afloat, about a bomb that is statistically nuclear. I do not know much of it; I was told it could destroy mountains." "Why did you not tell the members?"

"I was told not to," the general said.

The Devil turned back towards the back end; he knew where an open window was at, chuckled to himself, though, "I knew bringing that Uranium to Earth would pay off, giving a toy to a little boy here, haha."

This membership is no longer a community and integration. Everyone wants to join the frail. It was no longer a clique; thousands of people have joined, but there were a few billionaire families who still control, through political risings, the jurisdiction of the way life is.

It was October 1962. President Kennedy had success with Cuba; the entire island was surrounded by most of America's military destroyers, aircraft carriers, and warships, not letting anything in or out. Lockheed U-2 took pictures of Cuba where it finally was filling large potholes where the Russian missiles would be launched. Nikita Khrushchev's strategy a political and military was a fake fold, a bluff where Kennedy won.

The meeting was held in New York, a mediocre building in Manhattan. The Devil loved New York better than Moscow or Paris, and it had a feeling he loved. The look of Manhattan and the global business that took place there, and the way people despise each other, oh so good! He thought, "There are more high military officers here all the time, so much the better."

Samuel E. Anderson, Lieutenant General, smashed his fist on the table in front of him, loud enough to quiet the crowd. "Welcome gentlemen, I hope you are all having much entertainment. There is much news I have been told to give you."

The Devil thought, "I wonder...I think the clique is only a couple of families have to find out where they are at. These members are in the thousands who have real control?"

Samuel continued, "As you all know, Kennedy took care of the Cuban crisis. One year ago, Russia unloaded the biggest explosion of humankind, October 30, 1961, in Novaya Zemlya. Novaya is the place where over 100 atomic tests took place, the same as our Bikini Atoll in the Pacific. Spies let us know that at least 10 of those launch sites in Cuba would have the same Hydrogen bombs inside their missile. Only hundreds of miles away from America. Some of those spies are no longer alive. That atomic was called Tsar Bomba, 3000 times bigger than killed Hiroshima; the mushroom cloud was 40 miles high. Buildings 70 miles away were destroyed, windows in Norway, 350 miles away were shattered."

"One big firecracker!" the Devil thought.

"America officers knew about Tsar Bomba 8 seconds after it went off, shockwave through the surface of the Earth told us that an earthquake took place in Novaya in Russia, but we knew through earth plates that this place is the last place you would ever have an earthquake. Within hours we knew this was a turning point for atomic potential and capability.

The biggest bomb before that was Castle Bravo in Bikini Atoll in March 1954. The scientists made mistakes; the explosion was bigger because Lithium Isotopes, Lithium Deuteride had extra portions in it, and bigger detonation. There was a security soldier on a warship 23 miles away when it went off; he turned around after the detonation and threw gamma rays said he could see the bones in peoples bodies, like looking at an X-ray." Samuel looked down and finished his coke whiskey in one big swallow. "The reason I am telling you this is that we are coming to the point that... the bigger weapon would kill us all. Kennedy and Khrushchev are meeting to eliminate atomic testing, thus, eliminate the use of atomic in wars, a peace so to speak."

"Oh my, the little boys are getting smart," said the Devil.

"I have been told...there will be a sort of...cold war," Samuel said. "Just for your information, there was a time in WWII that General Patton had written a letter to Truman saying that when he is finished with the Germans, he should continue and take on what he called the Red Horde, Russians. During the end of the war, Russian soldiers killed Germans and raped their women. Patton begged Truman to continue the war all the way to Alaska, but Truman thought the Russians were our friends. I hate saying what would be different if,...but I can't help but wonder if Patton had got his wishes. The Union of Soviet Socialists Union might be called something else, maybe owned by different countries. We can only dream."

"You cannot change the past," Devil thought.

"This...cold war, will be the between the tensions, geopolitical and politic of USSR and America. I believe it will have more spies than soldiers within it; money will still go into its center, its core, which will end up in our banks."

The Devil was waiting for the skulls, but it never happened.

"We are taking no questions; what I have told you is all you need to hear," the general said. "Good evening, gentlemen."

"No skulls," the Devil whispered, "Those hierarchy families are killing those who are not faithful; I can hardly wait to meet them."

In Tokyo, Japan, there is a half-island called Chiba, on a compact trifling corner called Tateyama where billionaires reside. On that corner, you are disdained if you have less than 100 million dollars. Finding these families who wish to control, establish and initiate life's jurisdiction and dominance was easy; understanding their comprehension and grip on everyday life for the common was a query and sometimes quizzing. It was August 2010 as the raven flew in, stood in the back of the Japanese garden.

There were several families available, Saudi Arabians, Japanese, Norwegians, Chinese and American; many children were there as well. Guards and security were at each exit and entered. The gardens were sinisterly beautiful with Japanese architecture; Nihon Kenchiku were along the south water and the center of the complex. Puja tables were lined up with servants bringing in food and Hakutsuru wine to please the families. One portion that stood out was a Norwegian family, sitting at their tables in Japanese culture, shoes off and legs cross, no chair, at the front of the table, the Father was whispering to his son on what needed to be done, the boy was 15 years old and had a look on his face like he would like to be anywhere but here.

The Devil was studying these families, giving himself tuition on what made these families click. "All their financial barriers were covered by lawyers and taken care of online. Caribbean Islands, Tokyo, Paris, New York, Moscow, and London banks held trillions of dollars for these broods, these menage nuclear families. Their control over life for the masses was somewhat limited simply by the number of people on the planet. They owned dozens of corporations which held hundreds of businesses; they would often lose a billion dollars, two weeks later they would gain 10 billion more." The Devil could easily see these families were starting to care less for money, So much financial gain; it was like going for a swim in the ocean instead of a pool, so much water, like money, you care less.

The Norwegian Father muttered to his son, trying to stay out of attention, consummated to his son to follow orders; the son did not want to be there. The mother was ignoring them both. Suddenly many servers started to clean up the tables, and several others were taking the younger children away to a building on the northeast side. A few minutes went by, a Japanese man came from under one Nara, "I hope you are all entertained; if you need anything we have not provided, let the VPN know. Your attorneys will let you know of any financial situations that occur, pecuniary resources, stock in trade, available funds, available resources, capital means, cash flows, working capital, and profitability; we are all very, very rich!" The families applauded.

"Evil and sources of menace, its what money leads to," the Devil whispered.

"Let us get to the point, why we are all really here," he turned around and snapped his fingers. Out of the Nara, nine people came out, three naked women with hands tied behind their backs, three Geisha girls holding the hair of the naked women making them walk forward, and three guards behind them.

"Interesting," the Devil thought.

The Geisha girls pulled the hair of the clothesless women, tripped them when they reached low tables, and strapped them down face down. The three guards were carrying scimitars; each had one. When the women fastened securely, the Geishas took a few steps back, stood by the guards, and waited.

A teenager from a Saudi Arabian family got up from his table, came forward with a smile on his face.

"This one has the Dillinger personality," the Devil thought," Born with it."

Another teenager followed him, a little chunky from America, had a confused look on his face.

Instantly, the Devil had an emotion come forward he has not felt in hundreds of years, sadness. He looked down at the Norwegian family, the father and son disagreement on the action that was going to take place. The son is the third one who is going to do this deed; it all makes sense now, a victim, a scimitar, and a deed! But the boy did not want to do it. It almost brought tears to the Devil, that boy is me, and his Father is God! I am sad; I do not like being the Devil; I am a Saint! But Father makes me do it, these humans!!

The Devil looked down at the Norwegian father-son; the Father was practically crying, I outdo it. The son got up and went over to the tables; the guards gave the teenagers the scimitar. The Saudi teenager took three hits to have his victim headless; it took the American teenager at least seven slices to remove his victim's head. The Norwegian son just looked back at dad.

"This boy is good...he could become a man of Ethics," the Devil wondered.

The Father was more than disappointed; his son is unaware of how much power he could have one day. His son looked down at his victim, back at dad, and then took one quick, massive strike and took the head off with one blow. He never gave the scimitar back to the guard; he walked back to his table and threw it on his Father's dinner plate, then walked to an exit, his mom followed. His dad sat there with a sinister look on his face.

The Devil thought the same thing happened to me 10,000 years ago, didn't it, Father!!

PRIMORDIAL INSTINCTS

Written by Darin Graves

THE RAVEN FLEW THROUGH A THUNDERSTORM, looked down, and could see Charles Miller. Past 2 am Charles was breaking into a Jewelry store, he was a destitute, penniless poverty-stricken man who lived by weekly checks in a downtown warehouse. Relatively uneducated, he learned from the streets. The Raven dove down into the alley where Charles was trying to quietly break glass to enter the jewelry from the alley. Small things were in his favor, because of the pandemic, most people were wearing masks which is he was doing, it was very dark in the alley, he sprayed the half-circle camera and smaller scale miniature light with a wasp and hornet killer which could be spraying over 25 feet. Quickly and silently, he used a screwdriver to break the glass and pull shards of glass away. Every now and again, thunder could be heard from the lightning from the storm. He then got out a cable cutter and started to slice through the fencing wire right behind the glass, away from rain as he was under a small roof covering which protected the camera from rain. When enough of the fence wiring was cut away, he stepped into what seemed to be an office.

"I must be quick," he thought. He knew from experience that every time you commit a crime, there are many faulters which you never thought of doing, and by the time you are doing them, 20 more faulters would come from nowhere!

The Devil thought, "Watching him do this deed is almost comical... he is serious..but..."

Charles used his Stealth Angel flashlight and swiftly moved as he could; he was surprised that the door was open when he went into the floor room; little disc golf accent lights were over the jewelry glass covers. He saw a green beeping light through the corner of his eye, "Shit," he whispered, thought, "Well, I have already hit the sensory beams; someone knows this place is being robbed."

"This person is uneducated, but he seems quite aware that anything could spoil your deed, your fun..." the Devil reasoned.

Charles pulled out a Ti bone hammer from the bag over his shoulder and jogged right by the glass-covered jewelry smashing the glass to pieces; he would go all the way around, one giant rectangle, then go around again to grab the jewelry. Two quick, coordinated scuttles around the floor, smash the glass, then grab the jewelry!

He walked very rapidly, splendidly striking the glass at its center, cracking it open to a thunderous shatter as glass hit the stunning explay of rings, necklaces, and Pandora bracelets. One after another as his eyes kept looking over at the flickering green compact bulb and thought, "Quickly quickly."

He made it all around the first time, breaking the fragile glass, leaving the jewelry open to wanting hand. The Devil contemplated amusingly," I am a little bit impressed, came in through the alley during a thunderstorm, as quiet as he could, had all the tools on his bag over his shoulder, sprayed the camera with a bug repellent, knew when the protection laser beam went off, he as obviously been here before because he knows the architecture of the building and is ignoring the more expensive jewelry behind the rectangle on the floor, too much time to open. Wearing a mask and glove dispensers is impressive, but."

Charles made it around the square, put his hammer in his bag, opened up another long zip to put the gems and precious stones in a separate pocket, and did not want the goods to be stuck in with tools. He started taking out gemstones, one area after the next. A little grin and a childish smirk were on his face as he went from one zone box to another. He was thinking and considering, "Wow, I hope my stunt pulls off got to be quick!"

When he was about halfway through the displays of gems, he heard a noise.

"God damn it!" he thought.

He was closer to the main door up toward the front of the store. A man came in and stopped; it was crystal clear to Charles that this person was unaware that this place was being robbed. It was dark, but a few smaller lights reflected the jewelry that was still bright. The man took a step forward and screamed, "What…" It was only half a second until he looked down at Charles. Charles never knew him but knew he was the owner of this establishment.

"Exactly…exactly what Charles was thinking about before," the Devil conviction. "As a crime is committed, ten individual errors, botches, and confusions could happen, then after that, a dozen more!"

As the man entered the room, Charles's mind went into another altered state!

Only a second went by Innate behaviors and characteristics in humans that are not learned in any way; rather, we are born with them. Genetically hardwired in an organism and can be performed in response to a cue or prior experience.

Only a second went by. Charles never knew this man but had talked to him as a buyer of gems, I am under the mask, but he is not, almost primal thought that he knew this person.

Only a second went by, Pertaining to or existing at or from the very beginning, primordial matter, a response to certain stimuli.

Only a second went by......A thousand conceptions, concepts, considerations, notions, and thoughts went through Charles's brain, the experiences of his life, bad mistakes, and bad luck hold hands.

Only a second went by. Such psychological behaviors are called instincts, and physical manifestations of the instincts are called "mental reflexes."

Only a second went by Charles's "mental reflexes" was grabbing the 9mm from the back of his pants and shooting the owner three times in the chest.

Only five seconds went by. Charles went around the cabinets in front of him and ran through the front door. Hi primordial instincts, after all, was done, kill and run.

The Devil was hidden in the back of the chamber, though," " I really did not learn too much," he was so predictable. "If anything, it was concrete evidence of how people run their lives." There is no answer to the question, The meaning of life?

PRESENCE

Written by Darin Graves

IN 1971, TIMOTHY JUST HAD HIS 6th birthday and went to first grade, early November. His family had five children; he was the youngest, dad held a career and delivered financial gain while his mother raised kids. A small house, but the seven tried their best to be a normal family. His bedroom also belonged to his older brother. It was a Sunday night, so the household was in bed by 10:30, dad had to go to work, and the youngsters had to go to school.

Everything was silent, Tim could hear his older brother snoring, and about 10 minutes ago, mom had turned off the front room lights and had gone to bed. The shadows left things in the dark unseen, and sometimes unexplained. He was not afraid of the dark; he just concept obscure inexplicable sights and silhouettes left things baffling; his eyesights give more questions than answers. He had always thought that design, that simple suggestion for years after what he had seen that night. Everything was in shadows, black and white, as he looked through the room. There was a window across the other side of the room above his brother's bed. Through the thin curtains, it let in outside light, small as it might be, to give shadows and a cloudy, gloomy look to all objects inside the room. It reminded him of The Twilight Zone that his brother and he saw earlier just that night. The minutes went by as he was looking forward to first-grade class. He liked his teacher, was sound, and even with her students. Every now and again, he would hear small noises; it would resonate through his mind; it was nothing, a bug, a mouse creeping in the shadows. It was really nothing...but... When the presence showed itself, it made no noise. Tim thought that mom had gotten out of bed, looked through the half-opened door but saw no light. Tim looked back at the wall at the end of his brother's bed and saw the light coming out from it, made the shape of a man standing there. It was like a shadow, and only it was light; instead of a shadow-blocking light, the light was coming from it. The man started walking; there was really no fear in Tim; the presence never looked at him as it walked by, his brother still snoring. The presence disappeared through the door, and everything was dark again. Tim got out of bed and opened the half-closed door, saw nothing, silent shadows only. The night has a special glow to it; everything is black and white; fear was finally getting the better of him; he dove into his bed and hid under the covers.

Years had gone by, Tim never really talked about his vision, the phantom, the wraith that he saw as a kid. Every once in a while, during conversations of the strange, he would mention that he saw a ghost. What he did not talk about were the nightmares, a tribulation of horror. It was an illusion that they were nothing but. The tormented night terrors were real; he remembered how he was not afraid as the presence walked by, never looked at him, did not really care; the phantom in his dreams was hideous, tense, and disagreeable; they were there to petrify and shock you. He was always 10 feet away from the door of their house, the night foggy and dark. He looked around; the thick fog had everything dismal. It was the same nightmare, over and over again. Why did he do the same thing all the time? Run from the house, do not go in; his aspiration never came true. Could I actually think inside my night horror? It was like a hallucination; I did the same damn thing every time, walked into the house knowing the fear was waiting for me. I walked in through the dark, sinister house, and no one was there. I walked past the front room, the kitchen toward the hallway, stopped, and stared at the door which leads to my room. Hands shaking, couldn't blink, don't go in, don't go in, but I did just that. Step after step towards my own bedroom, hands still shaking, no noise, but I knew it was there. Slowly opening the door...knowing it was there. It was almost pitch black in there; the room felt unlit and inky. A few seconds went by... then I saw it, a small light from the wall, the same wall it came out when I was a kid, it took the shape of a man standing there, the difference from the dream as a kid was his face, he never looked at me the first time, he had a smile which turned into a grin, a smirk with fangs. He was looking right at me. Slowly he lifted his arms; giant talons grew out of each finger. His grin turned into a wide-open mouth...he started screaming! It was almost canine....clapperclaw...jaws went into a muzzle... fangs revolved to daggers! He started to float, 6 inches, maybe a foot from the floor... and began levitating my way. The scream, oh God, he is floating right at me! The shriek turned into a howl, bellowing me to fear! Its mouth was wide open to swallow me.

I let out a cry as I woke up, sweating in my bed. It was Tim's third year at college, lived in an apartment six blocks away from campus. The clock told him it was 3:48. Why, why the same nightmare every time. Tim sat there thinking of the nightmare; nothing is ever too altered, night, our old house, foggy night, I go in and see the specter, the presence that haunts my night sleep. What could I possibly do to change this?

Again, years have gone by, Tim would sometimes share the time he saw an apparition, but he kept the nightmares to himself. A couple of months would go by before he would have the classic slow-motion hauntingly inexorable horror dreams, some times he would forget about them, have a good night's sleep, but most nights, he would wonder, will I have the perpetual and horrible terror tonight?

Tim moved to a suburb of the twin cities, started a career in sales, sold commercial advertising for a paper. He got along with his co-workers and management for the company. He was enjoying his life there and was looking to buy a house, tired of apartment life, get rid of the cluster mess. It was a Friday night, and he did not go to bed until 1 am. The nightmare was a little different this time. Outside of his old house in the little town, he grew up in, night and foggy like usual. Ten feet away from the front door, no one around. He could actually feel fear in himself as he slowly walked to the front door. Nothing is different so far. He silently opened the front door, crept in, went through the front room and kitchen to the long silent hall. Dark and shadowy, the hall had a mist covering the floor. Don't go in. don't go in, but I did. The bedroom was full of shadows and things that go bump in the night. The slightly moving visions were macabre and disturbing! Was it an illusion, or was something coming at me? My black and white vision saw small objects on the floor move, or were they only sitting there? The man never came out of the wall across the room; he was standing right next to me!! I slowly looked to my left; the sinister smile on his face turned into a grin, opened up wide as he started screaming, inches away from my ear. I couldn't close my eyes; the shrieking screaming was bellowing me to fear and panic!

Couldn't move; the howling scream was so loud you couldn't hear mine! I stood there for several seconds, was immobile, locked, and stuck in space; the presence next to me wanted to devour me! Screaming, raging, eat my flesh and spit me out! The presence came fourth and big chunks of my face. Pain? Is this possible? His dagger claws sunk into my neck, making blood flow across the room. He bit into me only a second when I woke up with my scream in my apartment building, and sweat was dripping.

Months later, Tim was putting forth a proposal for an Auto company he had done business with. He ran into a fellow worker and friend, Daniel.

"Hey Dan, are Joe and the bigger bosses around? I have a Client ready to put lots of money in to make more sales," Tim asked.

"Yeah, they are around. They are in a meeting right now, so I would wait a little bit," Dan replied.

"Are you finally buying a home?"

Tim replied, "Yes, nice home in a safe and beautiful area about 10 miles away from here, so it will be an easy drive from here to my house. I should have you come out and take pics for me. Do you have a second job with that camera of yours?"

"I have had many jobs before taking pictures before this job, and now I shoot just for fun," Dan said. "Hey, I have seen some of your writings you put in for ideas for marketing; you are talented, some of those small-scale compact schemes can turn into major projects. A little idea becomes a big idea."

Tim was liked in this position for this company; he had given marketing proposals and suggestions to other salespeople. He did something he promised himself he would not do; he wrote a comical one about seeing a ghost for a pitch for buying. "Dan, did you see that one about a glimpse of the spirit, of a ghost, but because?"

"Yeah, that was the only weird one you have; the rest are great; you wrote on the bottom of the proposal that you have actually seen a ghost. Why?"

Tim got shaky, thought just keep it to yourself, but he couldn't, "I saw an apparition when I was a kid, sounds weird but true, I sometimes have... nightmares about it, reminds me it actually happened."

Dan had a peculiar, curious look on face, looked both ways down the hall, took a step closer to Tim, "A couple of years ago, when my wife and I went to Utah, Zion national park, we were hiking through some of the hills on the south side, just strolling along enjoying the wilderness, I heard a strange sound, looked down at a log...it had a face on it, a moving face which was looking at me. I looked up at my wife, who was looking away; I looked back at the log, the face moved up a couple of feet, still looking at me. I was petrified, and I told my wife I had hurt my ankle, went back to the campsite, put everything in the truck, and went to a hotel, did not want to sleep there ruined that trip."

Tim said, "I guess I am not alone."

Dan explained, "Not alone at all, man; everybody has a secret."

Tim spent the next weekend running errands, groceries, a doctor's appointment, and cementing final details about his new house; he went to bed around 11 pm Sunday. Sometimes he thought about his night terrors before bed, but usually, it was not thought of. Tonite was no exception; the nightmare was true to form. He was on the sidewalk in front of the house he grew up in, turned, and looked at the house, dark night with thick fog all around. He looked at the windows, pitch black. There really was no thinking, just a heightened sense of awareness; I could not stop what was happening, walked up to the front door, and went in. The colorless aroma of the darkness, the movement of the mist on the floor made the house was aware, alive. Through the front room and kitchen, silence. The hallway seemed like a mouth; I was being swallowed whole. The door to my bedroom was like a tongue, tasting me as I was consumed. I went into my bedroom, ugly, dark, and sinister; the presence had not shown himself yet. A bit of light coming in through the window made sure everything was not pitch black. The hazy smog on the floor hid certain things. It was almost up to my shins; it disappeared right at my feet, there it was! The face gaped at me; the manacing threatening smile turned into an ugly frown, razor-sharp fangs could be seen as it started to scream! It was on the floor right at my feet, balefully glancing at me. Its hands came out of the floor next to its face. Nothing could be heard but its scream as it was levitating out of the floor right in front of me! It could almost feel like you knew you were asleep but starting to sweat. It raised out of the floor in front of me. Its hands went right around my neck, and its fangs bit me in the face!

I put my hand over my heart as I woke up, let out a screech then a sound of relief. What could I do to stop this? See a Psychiatrist? A comical thought went through his head, can Ghost Busters provide help, "Ah yeah, I keep having these nightmares" He felt like he was caught in a trap, the nightmare was the same but a little stranger every time, it took him by surprise, months go by but it comes back again. Is there anything I can do to help myself?

A couple of weeks later, he ran into Dan again; Dan came into his teeny office, "How is it going, Tim."

"Good, nice to see you; what's up" Tim replied.

"My wife and I are going to try a new type of business; she is tired of me taking thousand of photos just for the thrill of it. She thought that I could take people's images, their thinking and messaging and notes and put them with my camera eye, and put a photograph with what they are analytically writings by a picture. You are my guinea pig, first one; what do you think," pulled a book out of his bag and handed it to Tim.

The book was entitled Tim's Writings, "Wow, thank you" Tim opened it and saw pictures from Mount Rushmore National park, Museums, pictures of Alaska, a skating rink, a football team, photos taken from high towers and the bigger city they belong in. Each with a writing, small or short, from Tim. "Damned good idea, I am impressed!"

"I got most of the writings from your ideas and individual thoughts from the writings you left for the salesman, combined with some of the stuff you told me; I hope you like it, sir; I have a meeting with a client in a bit, have to get going, let me know what you think."

"I will do just that," replied Tim.

Dan was already out the door, "Give me a call; leave a note if I don't answer."

Tim looked toward the back of the book, the time he saw a specter was in there, a photo of an old house. "Damn," he whispered.

Tim was like most people, hated moving. He had help from his sister and a couple of strong nephews. All the smaller stuff was in boxes, and bigger stuff was disassembled, trying trying to make a hard job easier. His sister Sheila saw the book he got from Dan.

"What's this,... Tim's writings. Hmmm," She looked through it, changing pages.

"Yeah, I got that from a friend from work; he takes individual thoughts and writings and puts them with a photo of his own; I think he might try to start a business with it. We need a break. Want a Corona?"

"Yes, please," said Sheila as she was enlightened by the book. Tim got out a couple of beers and sat down.

"This is really awesome, incredible pictures," Sheila said as she was slowly going page to page. The nephews were still loading up the truck as Tim and his sister was resting their backs.

Suddenly, Sheila looked at Tim with a perplexing glare, "This last note here...from you.. says you saw a ghost in our house...how old were you?"

Tim thought immediately about the demon in his dreams. Why would she ask that? "I was six years old. Why?"

Sheila was six years older than Tim, "I remember that time when dad told me...the owner of the house before us...hung himself...in that house."

Mayhem, confusion, disorder, chaos, pandemonium filled Tim's mind. A normal day turned to disarray. Tim waited over 40 years to hear the truth finally come out! "I have to go to the bathroom" when he got in there, he put his hands over his face, stay calm, gets the move done, and forget about this entire thing, but he couldn't.

His first night in his house, a ton of work still had to make it a home, obstacles had to be put away in proper order, but the bedroom was done first. He was unaware of the house's past, and the former owner committed suicide in that house. The nightmares went on and on until Tim knew of the ugly history of his childhood home. Had a coke and whiskey before he went to bed. The chaotic nightmare was waiting for him. This time there was no fog; he was in front of the house, everything seemed different. It was night, but the street corner lights were on. He went inside the front door, no mist. Tim walked back to the hall, silence. When he opened the door, the presence was standing right in front of him. They looked at each other, a small smile on his face. He walked right by me as he did when I first saw him as a kid—no uneasiness, just…calm.

A year has gone by; Tim had to travel back out west, stopped by to see his brother Curt and some other relatives. Never had another nightmare since the last one, the calm one. He was in the town he grew up in Saturday morning when a thought occurred, and I wonder if the library still had archives of the past in italics. The library was still in the same place; Tim parked right outside and walked around the corner to the lower aisle; he walked up to the front desk to the librarian...odd! A short guy in a three-piece suit with a bowler hat on had a sharp mustache and a small beard. Ok...strange.

"Hi, I was wondering if the library still contained old archives of the cities past, all the old newspapers on italics or film," Tim said.

Lucifer looked at Tim, a little smile from the Devil, "I believe we do have what you are looking for," very neatly, Lucifer gestured his arm right behind him where there were small drawers and rolled film covered the desks behind him. "What are you...looking for?"

Tim thought this was an odd situation, this weird librarian. I should not even be gesturing this past. "This is kind of...odd, I was looking for... this happened so many years ago, you probably don't have it, over 50 years ago."

"You would be surprised," the Devil taunted. "I am looking for," Tim said.

The Devil had a grin, half-smile, half-knowledge, "An obituary, a funeral?"

Tim was shocked, though, "How the hell...does he know this?" Said, "Yeah, I am trying to find information about my past."

"About...hmm 50 years ago, give or take?" "Yes," Tim said.

The Devil scrolled through different drawers, looked back at Tim, a creepy smile on his face, "I think I found it."

"I did not give you any fact or information about what I am looking for, you have no clue what I am looking for, and yet you found it?" asked Tim.

"Trust me. Take this film over to the screens and tell me this is not the film that shows what you are looking for."

The Devil gave Tim the film and pointed to desks that had film screens. Tim slowly walked over to the desks, turned on the lights, and shoved in the film through the side. He looked back at the librarian; he was gone. This is so freaking weird. He turned the circular knob which pulled the film through. He glanced back, no librarian. "Weird," he whispered. It went right to what he was looking for, the actual address and a picture of the house, August 1960, Charles Larsen read the story. Charles was never married, had several girlfriends who disappeared. He was never arrested because there was no body found. He hung himself in the front room.

"Life can be so strange," he thought; hopefully, my nightmares will come to an end. This story was so huge in my life—hopefully, no more nightmares.

COUNTERPART

Written by Darin Graves

FROM THE BOWELS OF HELL, SATAN was directing his own thoughts. He looked through the walls and caves and hollowed gallery of the underworld. Melting liquid grid on oils loins can fuse flesh to gas; no pain just feels warm as you are liquified. Freezing the flesh is just as potent, normal temperature to glacial ice in seconds. There were a thousand souls; the abode of the dead was lingering in Purgatory. Naked, they watched and looked at each other as they felt pain, remembering what they did as humans to bring this upon their souls.

"Don't worry, children, and your pain will only last as long as your sins," the Devil thought, "You will see other planets, other galaxies when your sins have been nullified."

The Devil has a problem; he is quite aware that Father will have Jesus Christ make a second appearance on Earth; as such, he must make sure the Devil's counterpart will be ready for the challenge. He will make sure the AntiChrist is intelligent, wealthy, connected to political agents and officers, ready for the task, and hidden. He has to find the proper mother for this to happen.

John 14: 1-4 "Do not let your hearts be troubled. You believe in God; also believe in me." Behold he cometh with clouds; and every eye shall see him, and they which pierced him; all the kindreds on Earth shall wail because of him. The second coming of Jesus Christ is the hope of believers that God is in control of all things and faithful to the promises and prophecies in his word. "Jesus wept."

Lucifer can feel the presence of Jesus, and his pure faith and belief lead men to reliance and conviction towards heaven and God, our father. The AntiChrist must have the ability to rule men, control the jurisdiction and sway the masses of his dominance while still hidden away from those who see righteousness as their calling. "It will be hard to find the women who will raise my son to the dominion of all he sees," Devil thought.

Manhattan, 1.6 million people on an island, the crow flew down across massive buildings with people who are of various types of religion and backgrounds, most of which are atheists, do not believe in deities. Lucifer flew in and had to go down several flights of stairs to find what he was looking for. "The average human," he conceived, "loves his own torments... celebrates, amuses, gratifies, musing his personality." He looked around, beautiful women in floating cages satisfying men around her by dancing and showing flesh. The bars were 100 feet across, filling and intoxicating the caste of people. Father? Are you watching this? Dressed up, three-piece suits, gorgeous dresses, some half-naked, gays, some into BDSM, all were here.

At the end of a bar, he found her, Mary Wright. She loves going to places of this nature, loves watching individuals amuse themselves, and likes the music they play. She is very aware of her shape, never drinks alcohol, is addicted to the gym, and watches her weight. She has won beauty pageants before. She entertains herself by watching fools; she sometimes sees herself as a black sheep of her family because she is 34 years old and does not want to get married and have children, as mom wants her to do. She is financially wealthy, like the rest of her family, 62 million last time she looked. The Devil knew she was related to some liberal-minded democrats who could push individuals into power in a heartbeat, "Fucking democrats...yes, my son will be hidden."

"Excuse me," Lucifer said, "Could I buy you another pineapple slushy, Mary." Mary looked at Lucifer, waited several seconds, "Who are you, and why do you know my name?"

"Oh Mary, I know much about you,..of all the men in this place who have hit on you, you laugh at, all they want is you in bed." Lucifer raised his hand; he was tired of being here already; he moved his fingers to catch Mary's attention, hypnotizing her, inducing a calm, focused state, raising the smoking gun of awareness of his own thought into hers. Mary looked at Lucifer, "I am aware of your family past," the loud music seemed to disappear to Mary, "You are unaware of who you really are, you have asked if you are a lesbian, you have asked if you are a Sub for BDSM, you have asked yourself if I should have kids..all these moments will come to nothing...I have an answer for you, what you really should do with your life."

Mary's eyes were wide open; she was half-aware that she was mesmerized by this short guy in a suit; she raised her own hand and touched his. "I don't know you....but I feel as though you know me...I always ask myself questions about who I am and what quests does my life has for me."

Their hands held each other, "Let us go back to your place and discuss our future," Lucifer said.

"Yes, let's."

It took only 15 minutes to go back to her apartment, and she had the 52nd level to herself. Giant rooms and hallways, windows on the south side showed Manhatten and half the water surrounding it, dazzling magnificent view. Mary was observing the beautiful field of vision, "I love this view…

It sometimes gives me peace," she turned to Lucifer, "You were talking about. our future?"

"Yes," Lucifer did not have to go any further; their minds fused with each other; he put his left hand under her skirt, fingers over her underwear and softly touching her clitoris. "I want you something better than what you have had before; I want your future to raise a son who will be like no other; this planet will be his kingdom. All men will do his bidding. For thousands of years, he will rule political, social, and financial sectors and zones. It is my time and yours as well."

"Yes…Lucifer," they went into the bedroom; she stopped at the bedroom mattress, eyes closed. He never took his hat off, came up behind her slowly too off her clothes. Shirt, skirt, and underwear off. He grabbed her hair, pulled her head back, and could see she still has her eyes closed. Kicked his leg in between hers, so her legs were spread, touched her breasts, nipples erect. He pushed her down; her forearms were on the mattress while her legs were still standing up, spread. He penetrated her.

She was lying naked on the bed; Lucifer put his lips right up to her ear, "Your future just started; you will have a son. Protect him, educate him, show him the world and teach him that all will be at his minions, hide him from his enemies, there will be many men who might know what his potential is, he must be protected until he can protect himself. This Mary is your future; he is your only decree. The sequence is in your hands; your motherhood can make the future. Our son will rule all."

THEY CALL HIM "LEATHER APRON"

Written by Darin Graves

AARON KOSMINSKI WAS A TROUBLED MAN. He was born to a Jewish family in Poland; he knew nothing but troubles growing up. He was bullied as a member of the people and cultural community of a religious rite. While growing up, he had a knowledge of human anatomy, started with killing animals as a youngster, found different organs that are considered vital for survival. He emigrated congress Poland to England in the 1880s. He worked as a hairdresser in Whitechapel in the East end of London, was there only a couple of months before many murders were committed, he was 23 years old and was seen wearing a leather apron no matter where he went. In that period of life, being a barber had some surgical knowledge to it, "barber surgeons" had an odd combination of bloodletting, dentistry, surgery, and haircuts, of course, did all the above. One of the common threads is a deep-seated hatred towards women, which could have been from withholding sex after rejection and rejection. He did not have a good relationship with his mother; he was never married and had very bad luck socializing with ladies.

Mary Ann Nichols was a domestic servant during the day and prostitution at night; she understood the degree of danger and violence in her profession but still did it. As a servant in the Wadsworth and other locations, she found paying to survive many more coins than she was making. Nichols was last seen alive walking down Osbourne street; the only light was whale oil lanterns at the end of the streets; she could not see the raven flying over her head.

The Devil winged and glided over Whitechapel for an hour; he went to human form and could see Mary Ann Nichols coming his way toward the gated stable entrance of Buck Row. Mary saw him and stopped, stared at him for several seconds, hair raising and spine chilling as the man only looked at her. She turned around to walk the other way and could not see Aaron Kominski standing there, grabbed Mary's throat and said, "Hello Luv," the Devil walked silently walked to the backside of Aaron, using shadows and fog to hide in, musing and reasoning to himself, "I absolutely must see this artisan, this craftsman, this mechanic at work, truly a must-see situation, he is the reason for policemen starting the "serial killer" outlet to describe and finalize and separate these murderers, there were many before him, but he is the first one that is socially remembered."

"Now then," Aaron said, "What is a pretty little girl doing up so late at night,...oh let me guess....you are...one of those girls...take care of man's fantasies for a coin." He was not forcing but still had a hold of her neck.

Mary has been in this situation before, "Yes...I will do exactly that," she quickly but softly moved her right hand to his bulge. He looked down at her body, "Do you know, my little Luv, what my fantasies are?"

She smiled, "No...please tell me.."

He smiled back, but it was more of the killer's frown, "My real fantasy... is this!" His hand tightened around her neck, pushed forward, and tackled her to the ground right next to Buck Row gates, yielding his six-inch blade. Mary barely got a howled cry in as Aaron pierced and probed the cutter into her throat.

The Devil stood there in shining prominent pride, joyful to watch the master do his work. He looked down the streets, but no one was there. Mary got in several cries and bellows, but they were decreasing in the tone for help. Aaron slicing carver opened up Mary from the neck to her lower bowels; he then pulled out biological structure, large and small intestines were grasped and put out on her shoulders. The blade sliced into her vagina, dividing and separating it too slippery tiny slabs. Then Aaron heard…a noise.

The Devil heard it too; through the fog and mist, you could see two shadows coming up the street. Aaron quickly stood up and walked away in the other direction, leaving Mary there to bleed in different pieces. Lucifer glanced at the atrocity, a twinkle, a grin at the first of the many; he pondered as he looked at Mary, "Oh Aaron, sweet, sweet Aaron, too bad your killing spree will be narrowed by yourself…your mind you are already losing sanity. Whitechapel is crowded and then some victims everywhere. Perfect place, but the timing has to be flawless."

The Devil flew away, flapping wings over Mary's dead body.

Annie Chapman was a flower seller. She was not happy about being a beggar, but did take financial part in her situation, had three kids, and married John Chapman. There was also no pride in occasional prostitution; on the 8th of September 1888, Annie she was doing just that, a dollar for pleasure. She was walking down Hanbury street when she saw a person coming at her slowly.

She, like many others, knew of the dangerous circumstances of that profession and was aware a dead prostitute was found a week before, but survival is survival.

"Hello gentleman, what are you doing out so late?" she asked.

The man stopped right in front of her, and several seconds went by as they glanced at each other. He replied, "Enjoying the beautiful evening. I should ask you the same question. Tell me luv what your motivation for being out by yourself is."

"Oh…you know, every now and again,..you can find a man who has needs," she replied.

"I see...a night girl. Well, I have a bulge in the rectal area that needs to be drawn off orally."

Lucifer was still a raven watching this. He saw Annie grab his hand and strolled, ushering Aaron into Hanbury street that had a fence coming out by a door, secluded and private.

"This won't cost you that much, mate," Annie said as she was undoing his belt.

"Good," he replied; he grabbed her hair and pushed her down toward his pelvic girdle; as she was going, he used his other hand to slice her neck with his blade. She stood back up and said, "No, no."

Aaron knew the area late at night, but there will still be around who could hear her cries. He wanted no witnesses, still holding her hair, the knife went across her throat several times, must be held noiseless. Lucifer watched him silence her leather apron, six-inch blade, powerful strokes as she fell to the ground; her head was close to the steps of the door of the building, the cutting edge of the biting knife ripped her midsection opened. Aaron did not like the situation, darkness was in his favor, but witnesses will still be close, finish quickly; he heaved out internal intestines and laid them across her breast and shoulder. He stood up and silently walked away.

Lucifer thought, "Another one another victim, poor Annie. It is only a matter of time before Aaron becomes more confused, with excessive fears and worries. He looked toward a window, could see the shape of someone looking out at the dead body. The raven flew away.

Elizabeth "Long Liz" Stride was a cleaner and immersed themselves in prostitution to make ends meet like hundreds of women. Whitechapel was full of the poor; poverty made the masses do the necessary to live. Everyone knew of the murders, but it still was not primary news, but Elizabeth tried to do her deed and make sure there were people around. She was by Dutfield Yard by Berners Street. As the sun went down, she was having a good nite, coins for oral. She loved the area because it had strains of different ethnic groups, and individuals casually walk by where there were still close hidden areas to sex work. It was a dark foggy night, she pondered, calling it a night, but there were so many men with needs. She perceived she heard the wings of a bird.

Lucifer landed on a tall fence by the yard, could see Elizabeth looking up. Right behind her, Aaron came quietly up and stood right behind her.

"Hello Luv, how are you doing tonight?"

She turned around, "Oh, hi there," Elizabeth said, looking at his leather apron, "Did you just get off work? Nice apron."

"Ah..yes," he replied, "Been a long night and I am so wound up,... satisfaction..is what I am looking for."

"Well, that is why I am here," Elizabeth said. "Come down here by these bushes, and I will give you that satisfaction...for the proper price."

"No problem luv, no problem." Privacy was about 10 feet away from the open, dark but no silent. Aaron peered and focused around him, no people, no witnesses. He reasoned they were alone. He conceived of ripping her to pieces; she was pulling up his apron to go below when he grabbed her hair, pulled her head back, and sliced her from ear to ear. She could only let out a half a scream; he half tackled her to the ground, a demonic smile on his face, raised the dagger, and suddenly heard a noise.

Lucifer saw three men coming down the street, half drunk and half ruthless, a portion of a gang on the east White Chapel area. Lucifer could read Aaron's thoughts; anger is growing, and he wanted to see Elizabeth's bones after he was done slicing.

Aaron stood up and quietly snuck his way between the bushes but was seen.

The gang member howled, "Who the fuck are you,..look at this man..." yelling at his other members, "An old fart sitting in between the bushes beating off," yelling back at Aaron, "Yeah...keep running motherfucker... come back here and we will rip you a new asshole. Motherfucker."

Lucifer could see Elizabeth, and both arteries slashed, dead; the gang never saved her but kept her from being mutilated, disfigured. He flew following Aaron, walking fast toward Mitre Square. Every now and again, Lucifer could hear Aaron mumble as he was quickly walking through the streets, "God damn it, I wanted to see her bones...argh..."

Lucifer was behind Aaron about 30 feet, turned into a man, a three-piece suit and a bowler hat following an insane man wearing a leather apron and a six-inch razor-sharp implement. It took a long time for Lucifer, but they finally came to Mitre Square, which was a woodworking warehouse.

Aaron was certifiable, and psychotic dementia was filling his mind with delusional contemplation, false became real, a conviction of what was false he thought was real. Demons became fallen Angels, and virtuoso made him dizzy. The innocent became sinful, disgraceful of what he thought he really was. He saw Catherine Eddowes and sprinted right at her; she never had time at all to protect herself, barely got in a loud "what" and then "no..." Razor splint across her throat, both went down to the earth, Aaron had her guts split open why she was still trying to scream for help, he punched his fist right below her sternum and tugged and dragged out entrails. The Devil watched her face as she looked down to see her innards being used as a toy; she looked away and started losing conscientiousness. "Oh Aaron...you are one piece of work," the Devil concluded.

When his knife was done, Aaron grabbed the shawl Catherine was wearing on her back; he laid it out on the ground while walking away. He got up to Goulston street toward the west and wrote down a message on the wall. Lucifer followed him close enough but still not to be suspicious, waited for Aaron to walk away. The Devil was jovial, cheerful to see what he had written; as Aaron jogged away, Lucifer went to the wall, it said, "The Jews are NOT the men that will not be blamed for nothing."

Lucifer was having fun, loved wearing blue swallow tailcoats with a cane-reinforced top hat, just such as the way London's police officers wore. He was whistling and hiding in with the rest of the "Bobbies," called woodentops at times, working for the New Scottland Yard, as he wished, no one paid any attention to him. He was there just to listen.

Sir Charles Warren had many articles to deal with, but the commodity and undertaking of the murder of prostitutes were high.

"Hello James," he said as James Monro came by his desk. "Charles, how is the wife doing?"

"Oh, she is fine," Charles responded, "To the point, how is the investigation going any culprits,..any delinquents?"

James answered, "Not yet, but there are several perpetrators in mind, there is a guy named Monte Druitt, have talked to him but certain times are in his favor, was not around when Mary Ann Nichols was slain, one of his best friends called him "sexually insane." A guy named Walter Sickert, an artist painter has time in his favor. You know how these judges work, Charles since we feel that the same person committed these murders, any culprit who can have an individual say he was elsewhere is all he needs."

"Yes, I agree," responded Charles.

"Charles, there is one guy, one perpetrator who fits the bill." "And… his name is, and why haven't you arrested him yet?"

"His name is Aaron Kosminski; there are witnesses who have seen a man wearing a leather apron around several of the murders, but no one has seen his face, nor have they heard his voice. We don't have enough to arrest him. I looked into his past the best I could. He hates women, was born in Poland, is a barber at a hospital, always wears his leather apron, no matter where he goes. Another thing, many witnesses see a man in a three-piece suit and a nice hat where ever they have seen Mr. Kosminski… two culprits?"

Lucifer was 10 feet away, making it look like he was busy on another desk; he tried no to giggle too much.

"Just stay with this Kosminski," Charles said.

"Yes sir, and one more thing, have never talked to him, but some witnesses say...well I don't know how to say it...they say he is going... insane, does not know right from wrong."

Charles looked up at James from reading the paper, "Good,..instead of having to worry about a sympathetic judge...we will just put him in a looney bin, Dementia and all of that, a lot worse than being in jail, I tell you that."

Mary Jane Kelly had no other jobs than prostitution; she rented a room at 13 Miller's Court, a place where the oldest profession was doing well. Aaron Kosminski is acting as just another individual, walking through the evening as anyone bristled and enjoying a nice evening trudge across the streets. In the back of his mind, anger, irritation, and vexation crushed any reason of thought. Deranged, mad and frenzied provoked him to lunacy. His last two victims never got the bloodied ripping they needed, the ones he so desperately wanted to give. His next victim will know the insanity of his delusions through pain and agony. The affliction of my labor will leave her fleshless.

"Hello Luv," Aaron said to Mary Ann as he walked toward the sidewalk she was standing on. The sun went down on the horizon; darkness was thick. "How are you doing on this nice beautiful evening?"

"Oh, I am doing ok mate," she responded, "It's a little cool out for my liking" Mary had knowledge of her craft, wanted to go inside for sex; it paid more than oral or hand. "Why don't we go inside? I have a room right inside this building; you can tell me your real fantasies where it's a bit warmer, we can snuggle and all of that."

"Oh, that would be perfect," he said, all the time I need for my deed, my labor, he thought. He considered and conceived his own thoughts; there is no reasoning; everything was diluted and grey, an overcast of misty thinking that was only half full. His past was even vague and pensive at best, "Mum never did me a shit load of good," he notion.

They went inside Mary's room, the first thing she did was light several candles. Aaron stood looking at her, his hand already on his blade, making sure the door was locked.

"So gov,..tell me, what do you want me to do to make this pleasurable for you?"

"Nothing," he replied.

"What, what do you mean nothing?"

"All you have to do is lie on your bed," he said.

These guys are getting weird, Necrophilia, she thought.

A second later, he hit her temple with the back end of his blade. She fell down to the floor, moaning. It took only a second to put her on the bed, tummy up, and put his legs over the top of her, one hand squeezing her neck, the other handheld the knife. He tried to reason with himself again. Were his thoughts functional? Vascular, neural structures were out of shape, senses were blurred, what is right and what is wrong? He could not grasp anything whole; some ideas were not one hundred percent. He was looking at her eyes, squeezed her throat until they finally opened. He started with her face.

"Quit looking at me; mum, don't look at me, mum."

The blade went down on her face 50 times, portions of the skull could be seen. Then the knife went from throat to vagina, using both arms to open her up. Like the other victims, he pulled out organs and put them over her shoulders. He leaned back to look at his work; his leather apron would need washing, dripping with blood. He looked up at the ceiling, rested his arms. "Everything...is not...clear," he whispered. He looked over at the only window, saw a Raven standing there through the misty lights.

He started laughing, got off the bed, and the laugh turned into a screech, a howl, as he grabbed the intestines and threw them against the walls. His blade was not done yet; he sliced the muscles and tendons from her hips and thighs, pieces of muscle were shredded one at a time, it took a little while to see the femur, but he had plenty of time.

He was almost done with his work; inside her ribs, he saw what was left of her heart, picked it up and cut off fat and veins that held it gaped at it, took a bite out of it as he looked down at a skeleton with some meat on it. Ripe was the smell, but he cared not. The myocardium or heart muscle was thick and hard to chew, had to bite it hard to be able to swallow. He looked down at the miniature bed that was holding Mary or what was left of her. Inside Aaron's mind was a series of cells that were unbalanced and unhinged. He asked himself, "Am I...mentally ill? mentally...handicapped?" He thought his mind seemed closed because his ideas and reasoning were never clear, perfect, or admissible, not one hundred percent. He made sure the door was closed when he left, tried his best to make sure he wasn't seen.

Lucifer knew that Aaron was going to insanity. The "Bobbies" will exactly do what he heard, send him to an insane asylum, no need for wasteful trial. Before Lucifer became the Devil, he would have been that magistrate who would have been open in mind, realizing that 90 percent of criminals were once victims.

I will write a letter to Sir Charles Warren, make him think it came from "leather apron."

Charles arrived at his desk Monday morning, bought a paper because reading it would be half of his day. A letter was sitting squarely on his desk; he looked around, opened it:

Hello New Scotland Yard; I was thinking about becoming one of you when I was younger, but the thought of being an officer of the law was a bit needless and worthless at a certain point; it's just not my idiom, not for me. Of the prostitution homicides that are filling Whitechapel recently... well, may continue, may come to an end, I have not decided what to do next. I am guilty of these crimes; Miss Nichols was; first, I left her body by Buck Rows gates. Annie Chapman was next, about a week after Nichols, I let her body "rest" on Hanbury St., Elizabeth Stride and Catherine

Eddowes were liquidated on the same night, that was a very substandard and disagreeable night for myself, I was not feeling the best, then there is Mary Jane Kelley, I had...time to deal with her. I will not get into the gore of these assassinations, and I can only think that this message is from myself and that you think, know I am the slayer.

Jack the Ripper

DEVIL AND FATHER

Written by Darin Graves

TIME AND SPACE HAD ONE THING in common; they were endless, limitless beyond the reason of thought, no termination, no border or conclusion. They were relative to, but not including matter. The combination of the three held things in the level, the way things are right now. Matter can not be destroyed or created; it will be there forever in different forms. Time is connected and correlated to matter; time goes by directly related to the shift and change of matter. As matter switches, time goes on. Space never stops; how much matter is out there beyond our observable universe, places our best telescopes can not be seen? Is matter relative to space, it never ends as well?

The Devil concept, "I am unaware of how far Father has traveled?

He created all; he could one hundred billion light-years from here and be back in a second; I have witnessed it. Maybe he is right with these humans." He was by himself at Saturn again; the gaze of the surrounding was extraordinary, there were so many moons, he could see Titan, Saturn's largest moon, which was a little smaller than Earth. "Those human beings use so much of their solar system, their Saturday was taken from Saturn; it was the Roman God of wealth," The Devil noted. "The rings of Saturn are from compact pieces of matter, comets, and asteroids with a bit of water ice on the surface, giving them the perfect light of stunning detail, so precious, no wonder Father loves looking at them, peace and mind of thought."

A look in the massive blackness, filled with suns and contrasting beams of light, still, the space takes up most. The distance of space between galaxies is enormous, yet these humans want to travel in space; one of their scientists was right; Einstein concluded that travel above the speed of light is impossible, travel to another galaxy? Huh, they can not even go to their own solar system without dying. Mars, Roman God of war this time, is negative 80 degrees Fahrenheit. Rely on your soul's humans.

The thought of Earth, such a slight trifling speck of dirt in the massive boundary of creation, what does Father think of these human beings? How far can they advance without killing each other? My Erudition of their place on Earth shows them endlessly flawed. They call themselves homo sapiens, anatomically consistent with Father's range phenotypes in their evolutionary strain. The Original sin is a Christian doctrine that humans inherit a tainted nature to prohibited reason to sin, born to sin? They will no matter what? Astounding!

The doctrine of sin is central in Christianity; the Devil pondered, "I have been witness to killings, wars, brainwashing, rapes, bullying, dominating and lack of ethics over and over again, from Adam eating the fruit to Adolph Hitler performing Holocaust on a religious freedom, it seems to never end."

The look of the "gas giant" Saturn was outstandingly admirable, angelic in its own way.

Crystallizing colors, graceful in so many ways, the beauty is almost appealing. Exquisite circles filled the surroundings of this gaseous planet; it looks like no other.

The Devil tried to defend himself, "Humans always use me and my ways, saying that the Devil made me do it, yes, I teach them that the gems and wealth and power can be found by doing things in a more sinful way. Sexual companionship, easy living, social approval, and being superior can be found by sinning! Hee haa, but when it comes right down to finding what you want in life is in you, not me. No wonder they are easily enthralled. They blame me for taking advantage of them, but no, I brainwash them with a diamond, and they want gold as well. It is what you desire, not me. And is that not the whole point? I fish them with physical desires; they fall into the trap most times. How can they advance as a whole when they are easily diverted and preoccupied with vague minuscule gadgets and false entities?"

Looking across space and the matter within it, a purlin of scantling rays and beams of light drew Lucifer's attention.

"Hello, Father," he said while gazing at a bright pearl of glowing light. It went onto a brilliant and intense marble that looks astonishing yet did not impair your vision.

"Saint Lucifer," I hope all is well," Father responded.

Lucifer was quite aware that Father went far beyond where Saints have been. Vast masses of space the Saints were unaware of Father called home. "Father, these humans on Earth always think you are present, but to me... you are never around, are you with them?"

"I am always there, their awareness know it with each one, in each mind, each personality there is a portion that knows there is a higher master. Through the evolutionary strain which I granted them, I can not control their future, which many pray for. They live their lives, their soul is their shield, their personal power, but they must obey certain orders; I sent my own son, Jesus for a reason."

"Yes, I know, Father," Lucifer replied.

Silence in the void, it is strange for Lucifer to look at the blackness of space and hear nothing; the blackness goes forever; only matter within the space gives it a soul.

"Your...erudition, your learning of people on this planet...have you been enlightened?" Father asked.

"Yes and no, witnessing their sins is always enlightening; they sometimes astonish me, but only to an end, the Christian Doctrine of sin and how you are born with it is stunning to me, upon them even it is impressive and yet bewildering. Like I said before, going fishing with a pot of gold as my bait, they bite every time, but there are still some of them with ethics, sometimes hard to make them sin."

"I know," Father said, "I have a minute more knowledge than you Lucifer, will they sin? Yes, will they stab their brother in the back? Yes, will they cheat on loved ones? Yes. But you see things in a small picture; the bigger picture is what you should look at Lucifer, humanity is a virtue linked with ethics of altruism derived from the human condition." Father's voice was so calm, "On their timetable, their news will tell of 10 people who were murdered at one time, an explosion that went off, people are saddened, but. Eighty years ago, WWII came to an end; 60 million people died, so they are improving on humanity. They still have a ways to go."

"A way to go and then some, you see the positives, I see the negatives, and believe you that I, yes I The Devil, did not create them, I merely put sugar on them, the sin is like taking candy from a baby. The one thing that disgusts me about humans, they have a proverb they use more as a joke more than its fruition; revenge is a dish best served cold; it is more of a comic relief than what it means. Being wronged by another human, burning a man's house down, or killing his only son, then you know pure hatred! Revenge is pure, and the perpetrator can not feel enough pain before he dies. Too often, they take things for granted."

Silence again; Father agrees with Lucifer more than he would like to recall.

"Father, their past does not matter; there is no time travel; it does not exist." Lucifer had a sad on his face, "Why did you give them a soul? They are so unaware of what you have given them, only if they see the struggles of your son, of what they could do with their spirit? Yet again, they are becoming atheists; they use their telescopes to see what they think is very far, only a glitch of what's available. Their dream, what I call a hallucination, is to travel from planet to planet, aware yet unaware of the challenges that exist. If they can make it to Pluto, the dwarf planet in the Kuiper Belt, without killing Earth with pollution and contamination, they would improve possibilities of travel. Rogue planets and some meteors could help as well, water and fuel. Space never ends, so their dream of worlds, a planet like heaven does exist, tenfold, their souls can make the journey, their physical existence can not let them try."

"No one can tell their future," Father agreed. "And you are right; they must keep Earth in reasonable favor, high esteem and good faith will assist them more than they are aware of. As their intelligence grows, their faith is the victim."

"As their observation, their intellect grows, they think they will no longer need a God, they are about to be smacked in the face, Father, you created them, there is no instant period of time where a lightning bolt enhances life as it hits a pool of water, that never happened, you gave them life and soul, and they stab you in the back for it! Was Jesus wasting time?" Lucifer had a clear questionable look on his face. "When they first try to go from planet to planet, they will be enlightened by the cost; space ships will disappear and never be heard from again, their imagination will tell them they could still be alive,..no, they will die in the void, no food, no water, no heat, no landing spots with what they need to survive. A question Father, did you make their planet and their existence, their bodies, to put in existing possibility of space travel, realizing they are close, but still can not do it, you play with them, space exploration and astronomy are oh so close, but the needs of their bodies outweigh the chance of advancing the project of travel?"

Father never answered that in time was a true response, a true retort to the question for Lucifer.

"What else did you acquire from observing humans," Father asked. "Like you know Father, not too much, my faith and education for this culture, their cultures are likely to what I expected, their sins, discontent with different societies, they want to dominate among each other rather than acting as a whole, they want to be rich, the average human has no perceivable ethics, they fight before they combine, quite simply they will kill each other before they would have the possibility of travel. Their little ball of dirt is being polluted and tainted and poisoned faster than they can advance. It was a little hobby of mine to watch serial killers and warmongers, my own tiny private gagrial. The clues were right in front of them every time, in one ear out the other. Their future is not promising, you know that as well as I, Father, the future for them get real, and you love them so much. You and I are going to watch them die."

"As I said before, Lucifer, I know them a little better than you," Father proclaimed, "You and I will watch them advance."

Lucifer had a questionable look on his face, "Their future is in their hands."

CONFLICTION

Darin Graves

GOD AND THE DEVIL, EVER TURNING Faith for and against. God created people; St. Lucifer did not like it. God designed, produced, and fashioned human beings the best he saw fit, giving him evolution through DNA. As the millions of years go by, only the fit survive. The only Saint who stood against people and God's creation, the Devil plays the puppeteer to push and shove into extreme sins, to do commodities, objects, and deeds to exploit for individuals to make their lives better. The Devil takes time to learn more about humans on Earth, his own Erudition, to gain an understanding of. Warmongers to serial killers, the Devil, does not like what he sees. For their coming future, see them die, polluting and corrupting the planet before they would ever travel to distant planets!

www.ingramcontent.com/pod-product-compliance
Lightning Source LLC
Chambersburg PA
CBHW021427070526
44577CB00001B/97